Four American Explorers

FOUR
AMERICAN EXPLORERS

CAPTAIN MERIWETHER LEWIS
CAPTAIN WILLIAM CLARK
GENERAL JOHN C. FRÉMONT
DR. ELISHA K. KANE

A BOOK FOR YOUNG AMERICANS

BY

NELLIE F. KINGSLEY

WERNER SCHOOL BOOK COMPANY

NEW YORK   CHICAGO   BOSTON

CONTENTS

LEWIS AND CLARK

JOHN CHARLES FRÉMONT

ELISHA KENT KANE

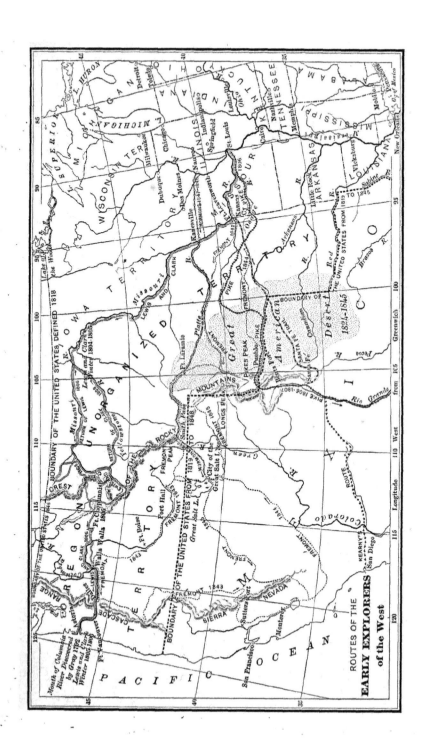

ROUTES OF THE
EARLY EXPLORERS
of the West

THE STORY OF
CAPTAIN MERIWETHER LEWIS
AND
CAPTAIN WILLIAM CLARK

Meriwether Lewis Capt.
1st U.S. Regt. Infty.

INTRODUCTION

The exploration of the Mississippi River was accomplished by the French a little more than two hundred years ago. La Salle, in 1682, was the first white man to trace the course of that great stream to the place where its waters flow into the Gulf of Mexico. Landing upon an island at the mouth of the river, he set up the arms of France, and took possession of the country in the name of King Louis XIV.

To the entire region drained by the Mississippi and its tributaries he gave the name of Louisiana, in honor of the king. This region included the greater part of what is now the United States. It extended from the Alleghany Mountains to the Rockies, and from the Great Lakes to the Gulf of Mexico.

The French made a few settlements and established trading-posts at different places along the Mississippi; but they never advanced far into the country that bordered it on the west. The whole of that vast region remained an unknown land.

Now and then the Indians who visited the French trading-posts would tell strange stories of a mighty river that flowed westward, of a lake whose waters were bitter with salt, and of a strange people in the Far West who rode on horseback and wore armor. But no white man had ventured far enough into those wilds to prove or disprove the truth of these tales.

It had been one of La Salle's dreams that a waterway extended from the region of the Great Lakes to the Pacific Ocean. He thought that such a waterway, once discovered, would afford a direct route across the continent—a route by which China and the East could be easily and quickly reached. For at that time nobody knew how far it was to the Pacific coast, nor was the great width of the western ocean taken into account.

After the death of La Salle other Frenchmen hoped to find that his dream was true; and the stories which the Indians related of a great river west of the Mississippi encouraged their hopes.

At length a French Canadian known as the Sieur de Vérendrye determined to explore the western country, and if possible discover the long-sought water-route to the Pacific. He had been for several years in command of a fort and trading-post near the head of Lake Superior, and the Sioux Indians who visited him there had related most wonderful things about the region which they said lay between their own country and the setting sun.

Anxious to be the first to explore that mysterious land, he laid his plans before the king of France, hoping to receive some sort of aid. The king was very much pleased, and was entirely willing that he should undertake the expedition at his own expense. He told Vérendrye that he might have the exclusive trade in furs in whatever country he should discover, but as for any further encouragement he must not expect it.

Like other explorers, some of whom have been more successful than he, Vérendrye was not to be discouraged. In 1731, with his three sons and a company of Canadian adventurers, he set out for the distant West. Early in the following year the party reached the western shore of the Lake of the Woods, and there built a fort. This was hundreds of miles beyond any other post or settlement that had yet been established.

Here Vérendrye remained for four or five years, trading with the Indians and exploring vast stretches of country on every side. In 1738, he pushed still farther west, and built a log fort on

the Assiniboine River. Troubles and disappoint-
ments, however, were constantly at hand: The
presents which had been intended for the Indians
were stolen, some of the men died, and others
were dissatisfied and rebellious.

In spite of all this, however, Vérendrye made a
journey southward into the country of the Mandans, and reached the Missouri River at some
point now in the state of North Dakota. The
Mandans repeated the old story of a great west-
ward-flowing river, and told him that, at the distance of only one day's journey farther west, there
lived a nation of men who rode horses and went
into battle with their bodies incased in iron.

After suffering great hardships, Vérendrye,
utterly disheartened, returned to Canada. The
work which he had undertaken now devolved upon
his sons. With their headquarters still on the
Assiniboine, they made various expeditions into
the vast unknown region towards the sources of
that river and the Missouri. On one of these
expeditions they saw the towering peaks of a
range of mountains, probably the Big Horn Range,
in what is now the northern part of Wyoming.

Returning to the Missouri, they buried near its
banks a leaden plate containing the arms of France,

and took formal possession of the country in the name of King Louis XV.

The elder Vérendrye, broken-hearted on account of his many failures, died in 1749, and a French officer of great courage and enterprise named Legardeur de St. Pierre was sent out to continue the search for the mysterious western river.

From the fort on the Assiniboine, St. Pierre sent a party up the Saskatchewan River to a point considerably farther than had yet been reached by white men. There they obtained a good view of the great mountains to the westward, and gave to them the name which they still bear — *Montagnes des Roches*, or Rocky Mountains. This was in 1751. Soon afterward St. Pierre sent out a second party; but it never returned, nor did any news of its fate ever reach the lonely post on the Assiniboine.

Discouraged on account of the many difficulties which he was unable to overcome, St. Pierre returned to Canada in 1753. The French and Indian War was just then beginning, and the exploration of the West was abandoned. For fifty years longer the vast region remained an unknown land, inhabited by wild Indians and visited only by strolling traders, trappers, and French voyageurs.

In 1803, Napoleon Bonaparte, who was then at the head of the French government, ceded the whole vast territory of Louisiana to the United States. The price which he received was fifteen

THE LOUISIANA
PURCHASE

million dollars. The region thus transferred to our government included all the country west of the Mississippi and between the possessions of Spain on the south and those of Great Britain on the north. It embraced the territory comprising the present states of Louisiana, Arkansas, Missouri, Iowa, Minnesota, North Dakota, South Dakota, Nebraska, Kansas, Montana, and Wyoming, besides a portion of Idaho and the greater part of Colorado, Oklahoma, and Indian Territory.

At the time this great purchase was made, Thomas Jefferson was President of the United States.

For many years Jefferson had had in mind the exploration of that unknown land. Long before it had come into the possession of the United States he had encouraged John Ledyard, an American traveler, to undertake such an exploration.

It was Ledyard's plan to reach the great West by traveling eastward. Sailing from New York, he first visited Paris, after which he

THOMAS JEFFERSON

journeyed through Germany, Sweden, and northern Russia, arriving finally at Irkutsk, then as now the most important town in Siberia. It was his intention to continue onward to some seaport in Kamchatka, and then to cross the Pacific to North America. But at Irkutsk he was arrested by

Russian officers, who carried him back to Poland, and assured him that if he again entered Russia he should suffer death. Disappointed, ragged, and penniless, he made his way back to London, and all his plans were abandoned.

A few years after this, through Mr. Jefferson's encouragement, another effort was made to send an exploring party into the regions watered by the Missouri. A company was actually formed, and placed under the command of André Michaux, a famous French botanist and traveler. But before the expedition had crossed the Mississippi, Michaux was recalled by his own government.

At last, however, the time came when the world should no longer remain in ignorance concerning the land that had hitherto been unvisited and unknown. Scarcely had the transfer been made to the United States before President Jefferson had perfected his plans for an expedition thither to explore its rivers and mountains and discover its hidden resources. By his recommendation this expedition was placed under the command of two young Virginians, Captain Meriwether Lewis and Captain William Clark; and before the summer of 1803 was ended a company was formed and on its way to the West.

LEWIS AND CLARK

CHAPTER I

THE TWO CAPTAINS

Meriwether Lewis was just eight months old when the first guns of our Revolutionary War were fired at Lexington. He was born near Charlottesville, Virginia, not far from the home of Thomas Jefferson.

The Lewis family was one of the most distinguished in Virginia, and Meriwether's father and uncles were noted for their courage and patriotism. All were wealthy and enterprising, and one of his granduncles had married a sister of George Washington.

From his very cradle the lad was accustomed to hear much talk of brave deeds done for the love of country; and as soon as he was able to run about by himself he began to show a daring spirit that was very wonderful in a child of his age. It is said that when only eight years of age he would often go out at night, alone with his dogs, to hunt raccoons and opossums in the dark woods. What a fearless little fellow he must have been!

In the pursuit of his game nothing could discourage him. Wading through deep snow and streams of icy water, and caring naught for storms or darkness, he would press onward when even stout men had given up the chase. And so it continued throughout his whole life: when he made up his mind to do a thing, he was quite sure to do it.

When he was thirteen years old he was sent to a famous Latin school in Charlottesville, kept by two parsons of the village. We do not know that he distinguished himself as a Latin scholar, but we are told that he had a great love for nature, and that the objects which he delighted most to study were the plants and animals of Virginia.

He left school when he was eighteen, and with a younger brother undertook the management of his mother's farm, for his father had died several years before. But farming was dull business for one of his adventurous nature, and before he was twenty-one he enlisted as a volunteer in the state militia.

Two years later he was chosen captain of his

company, and soon afterward became the pay-
master of the regiment. A young man who shows
himself to be both able and enterprising is almost
always sure of promotion.

When Thomas Jefferson became President of
the United States, he looked about him for a pri-
vate secretary, and could find no one better suited
for the place than Meriwether Lewis. It must be
confessed, however, that, with all his good qualities,
the young man was a very poor speller.

It was in March, 1801, when Lewis entered the
service of the President. He was then nearly
twenty-seven years old. Two years later Mr. Jefferson appointed him leader of the exploring party
which the government was about to send to the
Far West.

"I could have no hesitation in confiding the
enterprise to him," said the President. Why?
Because he was known to be a man of courage and
firmness and perseverance; because he was a born
leader of men; because he had studied the character of the Indians, and knew how to deal with
them; because he was a skilled hunter and understood all the lore of the woods; and because he
was honest, liberal, exact, and truthful.

Seldom has any man been better fitted by

nature and education for a great undertaking like
this. He needed only to learn the scientific terms
used in botany, and how to make such astronomical observations as might be necessary in describing his journey; and to acquire this knowledge
he spent two busy months in Philadelphia, re-
ceiving instruction from the ablest professors in
that city.

Early in July he was ready to start on his
famous journey. Astronomical instruments, presents for the Indians, tents, and various other supplies had been ordered, and these he was to find
at Pittsburg. The men who were to accompany
him were to be selected at various settlements
and posts along the Ohio.

President Jefferson was too wise and cautious
to intrust so great an undertaking to one man.
He knew that if Captain Lewis lived, all would go
well. But what if some accident should befall him,
and the expedition have no leader? To provide
against such an emergency he selected Captain
William Clark, at that time living near Louisville,
Kentucky, to be Lewis's companion and helper.

Who was this Captain William Clark?

He was the younger brother of General George
Rogers Clark, the famous Virginian commander,

who in 1780 drove the British from the Old Northwest and won that vast region for America.

William Clark, like Meriwether Lewis, was
born near Charlottesville, Virginia.   He was only
ten years of age at the time of his brother's famous
triumph, and before he was old enough to bear
arms the Revolutionary War was ended.

When he was fourteen his parents moved to
Kentucky and settled near the falls of the Ohio,
where Louisville now stands.   The place was in
the heart of the wilderness.   A fort was there,
and around it were clustered the cabins of a few
backwoodsmen.   All else was a wild solitude.

Young William had not the advantages of a
modern education, but he was schooled in the
rough experiences of frontier life.   We know very
little about his boyhood and youth, but that he
proved himself both brave and honorable there is
no doubt.   Before he was seventeen he was admit-
ted into the famous society of the Cincinnati, and
his certificate of membership was signed by General Washington.

At eighteen he became an ensign in the army
under General St. Clair, and at twenty-one he was
made a lieutenant.   When General Wayne made
his famous expedition against the Indians of the

Northwest, Captain William Clark went with him, having command of a rifle company.

When the Indian war was over he resigned from the army and went back to Kentucky. There he settled on a farm not far from Louisville, where he lived in quiet for several years.

To Captain Lewis and President Jefferson no other man seemed better fitted to aid in conducting the exploration of the Far West. Both were well acquainted with him, and they knew him to be a person of rare good judgment, accustomed to the rough life of the frontier.

It was at Captain Lewis's invitation that Clark consented to join the expedition. And late in the fall of 1803 the two men met at Louisville, and then went on to St. Louis with the little company that had been collected on the way.

In those days news traveled very slowly, and the French officers at St. Louis had not yet heard of the sale of the country to the United States. As winter was now setting in, the two captains with their party encamped on the east side of the Mississippi and waited for spring. The long, cold months were spent in drilling the men and in making things ready for the start as soon as the ice should disappear from the Missouri.

CHAPTER II

THE START

On Monday, the 14th of May, 1804, at four o'clock of a rainy afternoon, an odd-looking craft slowly entered the current of the Missouri River at the point where it pours its yellow, tumbling-tide into the Mississippi. This strange vessel was fifty-five feet long, and was propelled by twenty-two oars. It had also a square sail, which was hoisted when the wind was favorable.

In the bow and stern of the boat were little ten-foot decks with cabins beneath. The space between the decks was filled with lockers or boxes, which could be lifted up for a breastwork in case an enemy should attack the boat. Great boxes and bales of goods had been carefully packed below.

If we could have looked into these boxes, we should have seen clothes and tools, household goods and utensils, and great quantities of guns and ammunition. There were laced coats, cocked hats, bright feathers, medals, flags, knives, tomahawks, beads, looking-glasses, bright handkerchiefs, paints, gimlets, axes, kettles, mills, and various other things that were supposed to be pleasing to the Indians.

At the side of the large boat were two small rowboats. In these and in the larger vessel were woodsmen, hunters, guides, servants, and soldiers— forty-five men in all. One young man was in command. Along the shore two men were leading the

THE START

hunters' horses. Slowly the boats made their way against the strong current; but to those who watched them from the shore, they were soon out of sight in the mist and rain.

A rainy night set in, and the party landed and went into camp only four miles above their starting-place. The river's yellow, sullen flood rolled by them, carrying with it masses of shifting sands and tumbling tree-trunks. There was danger that these tree-trunks might come in contact with the great boat as it struggled against the stream, and wreck it with all its contents. This danger was increased because the boat was too heavily loaded at the stern.

On the next day, therefore, the carefully stored bales and boxes were removed from their places and shifted into the bow of the boat. This took time and hard work, but after it was done the little vessel moved not only with greater safety, but with more speed.

In the afternoon of the third day of their journey they arrived at the little town of St. Charles, about twenty-one miles from their starting-place, and here they determined to stop for a time. Here they found gay French people, living a careless, happy life, supporting themselves by hunting and trade and the products of their beautiful gardens.

These people warmly welcomed the travelers, and made their stay of five days as pleasant as could be desired.

Captain Lewis, who had been detained in St. Louis, now joined the party, and on the 21st of May the voyage was resumed.

For many days the explorers slowly worked their way up the river, passing creeks and islands, which they carefully described, and to which they gave such queer names as "Turkey," "Nightingale," "Lark," "Buffalo," etc., from the objects they happened to see in the neighborhood. While the boats moved slowly up the river, the hunters on shore were plunging through brushwood, clambering up cliffs, crawling into caves, and skirting prairies in search of game.

These hunters would hurry ahead of the party on the river, fix a camp, shoot, dress, and bring in their game, and then wait for the rest of the party to reach them. Sometimes they would leave the game dressed and hung on trees while they pushed on and made another camp still farther ahead. Sometimes a hunter would not be seen for days and weeks, and would be given up for lost. Then suddenly he would reappear, gaunt, half-starved, lame, and ill, but plucky and uncomplaining and ready for another hunt the next day. These French woodsmen and hunters knew how to find their way in the woods as naturally as they knew how to breathe. They loved the woods and would not be induced to leave them on any account.

Once in a while the voyagers would pass a

French trader's boat, loaded with beaver furs or buffalo tallow, on its slow way to St. Louis. The Frenchmen always brought news from the western country and had much to tell about the Indian tribes who lived there.

One of the first tribes encountered by our explorers was that of the Osages. These were a peaceable people who lived in villages and cultivated the land. Though courageous, they were less savage than most Indian tribes. They told Captain Lewis strange tales of their origin.

They said that the founder of their nation was a snail which lived long ago on the banks of the Osage River. One day this snail was swept by high water down the river into the Missouri, and after being tumbled over and over and badly knocked about, was left lying high and dry on the shore. Here the sun hatched him into a man; but he did not forget the home he had known when a snail, and at once set off to find it. But walking was hard work, and he soon grew very faint from hunger and thirst. Then the Great Spirit gave him a bow and arrow, and showed him how to kill and cook a deer and how to dress himself in the skin. So fed and dressed, the snail-man traveled on until he reached the home river-

bank, where he met a beaver. The beaver asked
him who he was and what he was doing, and
ordered him to go away. But the snail-man would
not go, for he knew this was his home. While
they were quarreling, the beaver's daughter came

out of the river
to see what was
the matter. She
offered to marry
the snail-man,
who accepted her
as his wife. Their
children were the
Osage Indians.

BEAVERS

Because they
believed this charming beaver to have been their
great-great — nobody-knows-how-many-times-
great — grandmother, the Osages regarded all
beavers with great respect. Until quite recently
they had very carefully refrained from harming
any of these animals. When the traders' price for
beaver skins, however, became so high as to be a
serious temptation, they could no longer restrain
themselves, but sacrificed their beaver relatives to
their love of money, very much as some people
who are not called savages are said to do nowadays.

CHAPTER III

JUNE AND JULY

The explorers did not remain long in the country of the Osages. On a bright June day they resumed their journey, the men slowly working their heavy boats up the river, while the two captains examined the shores. Sometimes they found curious rocks on which were painted rude pictures of animals or of frightful human faces with spreading deer's horns attached. The days were full of exciting incidents. The captains searched for salt springs; they killed rattle-snakes, gathered water-cress and tongue-grass, wrote descriptions of the country, and feasted on the fruits they gathered in the woods. Whenever good ash trees were found upon the banks, the men would make new oars. Whenever a strange bird or animal could be caught, it was "cured" as a specimen to be carried back to Washington.

For some time the party had no guide, but one day meeting some French traders who knew the country well, they persuaded one of them whose name was Durion to go with them and help them.

On June 26th the explorers reached the mouth of the Kansas River, and found there a country abounding in goats, antelopes, and wild turkeys.

Antelopes were then almost unknown, and Lewis and Clark observed their habits with much interest. They never ceased to wonder at the speed with which these animals could run and the great distance from which they could scent an enemy. It was in-

ANTELOPES

teresting to watch the hunters as they tried to catch them. Hiding in the long grass, the hunter would put his hat on a stick and carefully lift it up into sight. Soon the antelope, curious to find out what the strange object was, would creep up within range of the gun, and fall a victim to curiosity. Wolves would sometimes hide among the grass until the unsuspecting antelopes were close to them, when they would suddenly leap out and seize as many as they could.

On the Fourth of July the men celebrated the
day by firing off the little cannon at the end of the
boat. But time was too precious to lose in cele-
brations, and so their boats swung on past Gosling
Creek and Fourth of July Creek and Independence Creek, and the day closed with another shot
from the air-gun.

The July weather must have been very warm.
Almost every day men fell with sunstroke. Large
boils or carbuncles appeared on the muscles of
their bodies. To work the oars sometimes caused
great agony to the men.

The leaders feared the water might be bad.
They examined it, and found a poisonous chemical
in the green scum on the surface. Orders were
given not to drink the surface water, but to dip
deep and get the pure water below. Poor fellows
who were bitten by snakes were treated with poul-
tices of bark and gunpowder, which cured them
every time.

At last the Platte River was reached. There
the sailors carried out a curious custom. It seems
that the passing of the Platte River is regarded by
Missouri River boatmen just as the crossing of the
equinoctial line is regarded by sailors on the sea.
To mark the passing of it every man in the party

who had never been there before was caught and shaved, unless he could "stand treat" to his comrades. Near the mouth of this river a camp was made, and the party spent a few days in airing and drying their stores, which had been wet in many rains. They also made observations, drew maps, wrote up their journals, and prepared messages for the President.

Game was scarce, but Indians were not. Hoping to become better acquainted with some of the latter, Lewis and Clark sent out invitations to a council. After a few days the Kites, Ottoes, and Pawnees appeared to hear what the white men had to say. The Kites,—so called because they were always flying about,—were fierce and warlike, cruel to their captured enemies, and never known to give up a battle. Because of their warring habits they were few in number.

On the second of August, just at sunset, the captains were met by a party of fourteen braves of the Ottoes with their French interpreter. A council was arranged for the next morning, and an elegant present of pork, flour, and meal was sent across the river to the Indian camp.

The Indians returned the compliment by sending watermelons to the palefaces.

CHAPTER IV

THE FIRST INDIAN COUNCIL

Bright and early the next morning the whole party of white men was drawn up in line, in order to make a great impression upon the Indians. The Indians sat under an awning made of the mainsail of the large boat. Captain Lewis opened the council by making a speech, in which he told the red men that the United States now owned their land, and that their Great Father, the President, sent them greetings, good wishes, and promises of protection.

The six Indian chiefs said in reply that they were glad to belong to the United States, just as they had probably said they were glad to belong to Spain or France in years before. They asked for guns and ammunition to kill both deer and enemies, and asked for help in their war with the Omahas. Medals were given to the chiefs who were present, together with some gorgeous paints, garters, and powder. A United States flag, a medal, and some gay clothes were sent to the great chief of the Ottoes, who could not come with the rest. A shot from the air-gun put an end to the conference, and caused great alarm among the Indians.

The place where this council was held was called Council Bluffs, and the city in Iowa which bears this name, although not on exactly the same spot, derived its name from this circumstance.

PELICANS

Lewis and Clark were much pleased with the success of their first council, and breaking up camp set sail late in the afternoon. The following night was passed in a place so full of mosquitoes that the men suffered torments. Indeed, from the various reports of the men, one would think the mosquitoes were worse than the savages, and I am not sure but they were.

Moving on after a wearing night with these pests, the travelers passed an island where hundreds of queer birds called pelicans lived. You have seen pictures of pelicans, and know about the great bag or pouch on their necks. One day the men poured five gallons of water into one of these bags before it was filled.

Early in August they came to the burial-place of a great and awful chief of the Omaha nation named Blackbird. The chief had died of small-pox, as had whole villages of his people. He was buried sitting erect on horseback. His burial mound was on the river-bank three hundred feet above the water. He was a much feared chief, and the fear of him remained even after he was dead. Food was brought great distances by the Indians and placed upon the burial mound. On the staff above this dead warrior's grave Lewis and Clark fastened an American flag.

Invitations were sent to the tribe of Omaha Indians, of which Blackbird had been a chief, to join in a council with the white men. The delivering of these invitations was no easy matter. They were not sent by mail, but carried by armed men, who had to break their way through miles of thistles, tangled grass, and thickets of sunflowers. When they reached the place where the Omahas' village had stood, they found it no longer existed. It had been burned down after four hundred men and many women and children had died of small-pox. This horrible disease had probably been brought to them by some war party. Crazed by its awful ravages, the survivors had killed their

wives and children that they might escape a worse
death, and then set fire to the village.

Back of the ruins the men saw the graves of
the dead.   Hoping the Indians might hear of their
arrival, they waited
there a day or two.
While waiting they
made a kind of drag
of willow sticks and
swept the stream for
fish.   Their first land-
ing gave them three
hundred and eighteen
fish.   The second time
they drew out the drag
eight hundred fish

INDIAN METHOD OF BURIAL

came with it.   Despairing at last of seeing the
savages whom they sought, the men now set fire
to the woods.   This was the usual method of
invitation among Indian tribes, and was also used
by French traders to announce their arrival at any
particular place.

A day later some Ottoe chiefs with their men
arrived.   A friendly council was held, and after the
usual exchange of gifts the Indians rode away much
impressed with the greatness of the white men.

CHAPTER V

THE MOUNTAIN OF LITTLE PEOPLE

On a hot day in the latter part of August some time was spent in examining a queer mound and hearing the stories which the Indians told about it.

This mound was called "The Mountain of Little People." The young captains and ten men reached it after an uncomfortable walk of many miles. Indeed, the weather was so hot that even the dog was forced to return to the camp after going part of the way.

The mound was strangely divided and stood alone nine miles from any other hills. The view from the top was charming. Here the Indians believed the "Little People" or "Little Spirits" lived. They said these Little People were a foot and a half high and had very large heads. With sharpened arrows they killed any one who dared come to their mountain.

The captains and their men, however, spent several hours on the mound, and were hurt by no arrows but those of the sun. They carefully scanned the wide plain, dotted with herds of shaggy buffaloes. They examined the soil, gathered specimens of the plants growing there, and noted the birds they saw. But the heat on the hill finally became so intense that they were

THE SIOUX VILLAGE

forced to seek the shade of some neighboring bushes. Later in the day they returned to the boats, refreshing themselves on the way back by gathering and eating plums, grapes, and currants.

In the evening they set fire to the woods to call in the neighboring Sioux. In response to this invitation five Sioux chiefs and about seventy men and boys appeared on the opposite side of the

river and went into camp.   A boat was sent over
to them loaded with a present of tobacco and four
kettles.   Then the men gathered about the messengers who had just returned from carrying their
invitations to various tribes, eager to hear their
experiences.

It seemed that a village of the Sioux to which
they had been sent was about twelve miles away.
When the men arrived within sight of the village
the Indians came out to meet them and welcome
them.   They tried to carry them back to the village seated on white buffalo skins.   This the men
would not allow; but they were so hungry that
they gladly ate the good supper of dog's flesh
which the Indians cooked for them.

The men said the village was a very handsome
one, with its lodges covered with buffalo skins
painted red and white.   In each of these lodges
fifteen or twenty people could comfortably live,
since all their cooking was done out of doors or in
separate wigwams.

As the men listened to these stories the fire
burned low.   Then fresh logs were heaped upon
it, the guard took his position, and one by one
the tired hunters threw themselves down and all
were soon overcome by sleep.

CHAPTER VI

THE COUNCIL WITH THE SIOUX

When the heavy fog lifted next morning the party made ready for the great council. An American flag was brought out and set up under a large oak. A gorgeous cocked hat with red feathers, a laced coat, medals, and certificates were laid ready, and at twelve o'clock the chiefs arrived from across the river. Captain Lewis made a long speech to them, in which he gave them much good advice and information. He then smoked the pipe of peace, and gravely distributed the presents among them.

While the chiefs had been engaged in this council the young Indians had built a little booth of branches and leaves, and to this booth the chiefs withdrew to divide the presents and consider Lewis's speech.

Meanwhile the boys and young men entertained themselves and the white men by shooting at targets and showing their skill in many ways. The day was closed with a dance. During this dance

Lewis and Clark gave to the red men knives, tobacco, tape, bells, and other gay or noisy trifles, which they accepted with many grunts of delight.

After discussing Captain Lewis's speech, the chiefs made ready their answer. They said they were very poor and needed everything. They had no clothes, no guns, no powder, no shot. They were very glad to get the medals, but more glad to get the clothes. The English had once given them medals and clothes ; the Spaniards had given each man a medal, "but nothing to keep it from their skins." Now they were still poor, for while the Americans had given them medals and clothes, their children and squaws had nothing at all.

Other chiefs said the same thing, adding that they much wanted some of the "Great Father's milk," which was their name for whisky. They also promised to go to Washington to visit the "Great Father," provided a guide would go with them.

These interesting Indians were well built and strong, wearing the usual Indian blankets, much adorned with paint, feathers, and quills. Some wore necklaces of bear's claws, and all seemed brave and fearless; but there was one band of young braves who outdid all the rest in a strange kind of courage. These young men were sworn never to yield to an enemy, and never to avoid any danger. They did not protect themselves in battle. If they were crossing a river on the ice and came to a hole, the leader, scorning to turn aside, would march straight ahead. Of course he would be drowned, and all the rest of the band would follow him unless they were held back by their friends.

This seems very foolish to us, but it was courage of the grandest type to them. The young men who belonged to this band took higher seats in the councils than the chiefs, and in all their amusements and occupations they kept themselves apart from the other young men.

It was now September, and there were many signs of fall in the air. The heavy woods which lined the shores and covered the islands became brilliant with the colors of autumn. The acorns were falling, and great numbers of deer could be seen feeding in the open glades. The river became more and more shallow as the explorers advanced upstream, and much delay was caused by the boats grounding on sand bars.

Daily, vast herds of buffaloes and antelopes were seen. Many villages of prairie.dogs were also passed. These villages consisted of little mounds, and holes in the ground in which the funny little dogs—looking much like squirrels—lived.

The men once amused themselves by trying to fill up one of these holes with water, but after pouring in five barrels they succeeded only in driving out the distracted little owner, which they

caught. At another time they tried to reach the bottom of one of the holes by digging. After digging down six feet, they put in a pole and found they must dig at least six feet deeper to reach the bottom.

PRAIRIE DOGS

Soon after this a council was held with the Teton nation, which might have ended the expedition had not great wisdom been shown. After the usual speeches had been made and presents given, the explorers undertook to push their boats out into the stream. Immediately, however, at a signal from the Teton chief, an Indian threw both arms about the mast and refused to move; at the same time three others seized the rope which fastened the boat to the shore. The savages had determined to keep the explorers with them another day if not longer.

CHAPTER VII

AN INDIAN DANCE

Captain Clark made instant preparations for a fight. The small gun was pointed at the Indians, while they as quickly made ready their bows and arrows. Twelve soldiers sprang to the help of Captain Clark, and this act caused the Indians to hesitate and lay down their arms. They would not, however, shake Captain Clark's offered hand; but when he ordered the boat's small gun to be loaded, four of the Indians leaped into the water and swam out to the boat to talk with him. They said they did not intend to fight, but wanted more presents, and wished their squaws and children to see the strange boat. Captain Clark was glad to do this much to please them. So naming the island they were then near "Bad-humored Island" in memory of this unpleasant time, they decided to remain near the Indian camp over night and witness an Indian dance.

It was a wonderful dance. The great lodge of sewed skins was crowded full of red men. In the middle of the lodge sat the chief, with two little flags, one Spanish and one American, stuck into the ground in front of him. The peace pipe was placed on two forked sticks a few inches from the ground, and swan's down was scattered under it.

THE PEACE PIPE

When everything was ready, the chief made a speech, and taking up a bit of the fat dog that was cooking for the feast held it out toward the flag. I suppose this was an offering to the flag. Then he took the peace pipe and pointed it toward heaven, toward the four quarters of the globe, and finally to the earth, after which he lighted it and gave it to Lewis and to Clark.

The pipe ceremony being ended, the supper was served. Platters were set out and horn spoons given to the men. The flesh of a fat dog, some dried buffalo meat which had been pounded up and mixed raw with grease, and a queer dish of potatoes were served to all the guests. They ate all they could, and smoked all they could, but were glad when the dance was announced and the musicians took their places.

The music was even worse than the supper. There were men with tambourines, men shaking sticks to which were fastened rattling hoofs of deer and goats, and men rattling pebbles in bags of dried skins. This was the Indian orchestra; and when a chorus of Indian voices was added, the troubles of our friends grew almost too great to be borne.

And now the dance began. Indian women came shuffling forward carrying poles elaborately decorated with the scalps of the nation's enemies. Then Indian men came out, leaping and jumping and reciting the stories of their own brave and cruel deeds. Late into the night the dance kept on, but long before its close Lewis and Clark had gone to their boat, taking four of the chiefs with them.

These people had many interesting customs. Though homely and vicious, they were cheerful and happy. They wore their hair in long braids over their shoulders. These braids they cut off when a death occurred in the family. This they did in sign of mourning.

Their bodies were painted with a combination of grease and coal, and over their shoulders they wore a painted buffalo skin, the fur inside in fair weather and outside in foul. They wore leggings trimmed with the scalps of their enemies, and when in full dress fastened a skunk skin to each heel and let it drag behind on the ground.

They had a single policeman to whom they gave great powers. He was to guard the camp, and to give his life to protect his chief if the need came. Instead of a star he wore three raven skins fastened to his belt and sticking straight out behind. On his head was another raven skin split in two and arranged so that the head stuck out over the policeman's forehead.

After remaining a few days with these people, our party found it hard to get away. A battle threatened and was avoided. The explorers were followed for miles along the banks. Three times they were stopped and presents demanded. But at last the Indians were shaken off and left behind.

Farther up the river the Cheyennes were passed,

and after them the Ricaras. These latter Indians had their little patches of garden in which they raised corn, beans, and various other vegetables. They were kind to the old and never whipped their children. But they were said to be a treacherous race, and the explorers for a time felt very distrustful of them.

Their surprise when they saw Captain Clark's colored man-servant was very funny to see. This man's name was York, and his delight in puzzling the Indians was as great as their surprise at his appearance. He told them he was really a wild animal that had been caught and tamed. He frightened them dreadfully with the faces he made up and the antics he performed.

The Ricara Indians used no whisky, or strong drink of any kind, and they appeared to be much disgusted with any one who did. They gave Lewis and Clark handsome presents of corn and vegetables, and showed themselves generous and hospitable in every way. Many other tribes were seen and visited; but the weather grew cold and the ice became troublesome, and the explorers finally went into camp for the winter among the Mandan Indians, sixteen hundred miles above the mouth of the Missouri River.

CHAPTER VIII

WINTER AMONG THE MANDANS

The Mandan Indians welcomed the explorers with presents, and joined them in many friendly councils. While Captain Lewis was conducting these important ceremonies, Captain Clark scouted up and down the river seeking a good spot for the winter's camp. In one place he found no wood, in another no game. At last, however, a fair place was chosen, with five villages of friendly Indians within easy reach.

Some of the men began at once to fell trees for log huts. Others were engaged in building boats to carry messengers with maps and letters back to St. Louis. A blacksmith's shop was set up, and the merry ring of this blacksmith's hammer seemed to call the Indians from near and far loaded with corn and supplies. These they gladly exchanged for axheads, tomahawks, and bits of sheet iron cut into arrowheads.

Hunting-gangs were organized, and left the camp early each morning, returning at night.

Indians expert in woodcraft were hired as guides, and to the family of forty-five men was added a French interpreter with his squaw wife and family of half-breed children.

Indian callers were frequent. The chiefs came stalking solemnly in, followed by their wives, who instead of cards and card-cases carried bundles of meat and baskets of corn and vegetables. These gifts were for the white men. In return, the white men gave Mrs. Indian such dainty little articles as axheads, iron kettles, files, and corn-mills, which she easily carried away on her broad shoulders.

Almost every day large parties of Indians passed the camp on their fall hunting expeditions. Wild geese began to fly south. Ice came floating down the river. White frost covered the ground. Icicles hung from the trees. By night the pale light of the Aurora Borealis streamed above the camp, while the threatening flames of the prairie fire often startled them from their sleep.

These dreadful fires sometimes swept the whole country, burning to death men and women and destroying cattle. One night an Indian woman with her half-breed son found a prairie fire sweeping down upon them. Instantly she threw a fresh buffalo skin over him and fled for her life. After

the fire had passed, the boy was found untouched.
The Indians believed his life was charmed because
of his white blood. A tree left standing by the
fire they worshiped as an abiding-place of the
Great Spirit.

Neither prairie fires, scarcity of food, nor frost-
bitten fingers and toes kept back the work on the
huts. On the twentieth of November the camp
was finished, and named Fort Mandan. Surrounded by tall cottonwood trees, it lay on a low
point of land on the north bank of the Missouri
River. It did not look much like a fort. There
were two rows of rough log huts, with four rooms
in each row. Each room was fourteen feet square
and seven feet high. These two rows were joined
together at an angle, and thus the rear walls formed
two sides of a triangle. A row of stakes was
driven to make the third side of the triangle.
In the little yard made by the stakes and the
backs of the huts were two rooms for storing meat.

The hunters brought in the flesh of deer, elks,
beavers, and buffaloes, and the captains tried hard
to have the men take care of it. This they did not
like to do. They used meat carelessly when they
had it; and when they did not have it, they fasted
and hoped their luck would turn.

CHAPTER IX

INDIAN HUNTS

Those were great hunts they had in the neighborhood of Fort Mandan. Captain Clark went out alone one day and shot seven buffaloes. When night came on he was too far from camp to return. So he wrapped himself in his one thin blanket, heaped the fresh buffalo skins over him, and slept comfortably through a snowstorm. The next day he returned to camp and sent men out for the meat.

Of course our hunters shot their game, but the Indians had much more interesting ways of securing the animals which they used for food. Sometimes they hunted buffaloes in this way. A young Indian would be sent out to find a cave or crevice on the edge of a bluff near which the animals were feeding. Soon he would disappear. In the meantime other Indians would arrive, and carefully drive the herd toward the river. At a given moment the young hunter who had been seen before would appear at the head of the mov-

ing herd covered with a buffalo-skin. Carefully
he would decoy the herd to the edge of the bluff,

ONE METHOD OF HUNTING BUFFALOES

then he would drop into the crevice he had found,
while the buffaloes, frightened by the Indians
behind, would plunge headlong over the brink.

In this way hundreds of the great beasts would be killed. The Indians would take as much meat as they needed, and leave the rest for the vultures.

At other times the Indian hunters on their trained ponies would surround a herd of feeding buffaloes. Choosing one of the finest, they would fire their arrows at him until he fell dead. This they would repeat with a second, a third, a fourth, until their arrows were gone. The squaws who followed the hunt would then come up and dress the game and carry it home. Of course, no one could claim a buffalo as his own unless his arrow was found sticking in the wound. The game belonged to the one who found it. But this did not make much difference, for it was the custom when game was in any one's lodge for the squaws of the tribe to go and sit by the lodge door until given a share of the game.

In the spring the Indians would set fire to the dead grass on the river banks. After the fire new grass grew very quickly. This the buffaloes seemed to know at once, and would flock to the river, try to cross it on the floating ice, and either be shot by the Indians or, falling into the river, would swim and fall exhausted on the shore, where they were easily captured.

The way they caught goats was interesting, too. A large pen would be built, to which a lane of bushes would lead. Cautiously encircling the goats, the hunters would drive them through the lane into the pen and kill them at their leisure.

November passed, and winter, with the ther-

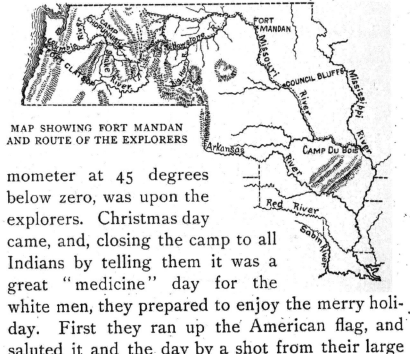

MAP SHOWING FORT MANDAN
AND ROUTE OF THE EXPLORERS

mometer at 45 degrees below zero, was upon the explorers. Christmas day came, and, closing the camp to all Indians by telling them it was a great "medicine" day for the white men, they prepared to enjoy the merry holiday. First they ran up the American flag, and saluted it and the day by a shot from their large gun. They then prepared and ate as good a dinner as the place afforded, and the Christmas festivities were over.

CHAPTER X

THE MANDAN INDIANS

These friendly Mandan Indians were really very interesting. They believed that in the beginning their tribe lived underground near a submerged lake. It was very quiet and dull down there. One day, however, one of their young braves found the great root of a grapevine that had pushed itself down deep into the ground. Seizing hold of it, he climbed up and up and up, until after a long time he came to the light. He looked all about, and saw grass and trees and animals and many kinds of fruit. He gathered some grapes, and then climbed down the long root of the grapevine and gave the fruit to his kinspeople to eat. All tasted it, and liked it so well that they began to climb the grapevine root to find some more. A great number climbed safely up to the light, but at last one very fat woman broke the root with her weight. Down came the earth and shut the rest in below.

Nine villages were built by those who had

climbed out. All the good Mandans still hope when they die to return to the ancient village by way of the underground lake. The wicked can never cross the lake. One old Mandan, who had lived one hundred and twenty years, felt he was soon to die. He asked his grandchildren to dress him in his best clothes, and carry him to a hill and set him on a stone with his face turned down the river toward the ancient village, to which he believed he would soon go.

All these Indians believed in a Great Spirit or "great medicine." Healing was their religion, and anything they did not understand was great medicine. Each Indian had his own "medicine." Sometimes it was a bag filled with strange things; sometimes it was a stone or an animal.

If any of the tribe wished to find out something of the future, a party of warriors would go to a great smooth stone, twenty feet in circumference, which they called a medicine-stone. First the men would smoke to the stone; that is, they would take one whiff and then present the pipe to the stone. After this ceremony they would go away into the woods to sleep. In the morning white marks would be found on the stone, and there was always some one who could tell what the marks meant.

These Mandans were brave and cheerful, and never complained. To make them more brave, however, they had one very strange custom. A young Indian would make a hole in the skin of his neck, pass one end of a string through it, and fasten the other end to a tree. To bear the pain without flinching was a proof of his courage. They were unlike many other tribes in their kindly treatment of one an-

A MANDAN VILLAGE

other. If a man was brought in frozen or injured, the whole village tried to give help. If one was lost, the whole village would turn out to hunt him. To the aged and infirm they were very kind and gentle. If a friend or relative died, a finger or a toe was cut off in sign of mourning.

There were plenty of occasions for mourning, for between the ravages of the smallpox and the devastations of the Sioux the Mandans, as well as other tribes, were daily becoming fewer in number. Whole villages were often left vacant. But in spite of their troubles they were a cheerful people, and found many ways of amusing themselves.

CHAPTER XI

THE WINTER

And so the winter wore on, with bitter cold days, little food, and many frost-bitten toes and fingers. Skirmishing with unfriendly tribes, trying to thaw the ice about the boats, treating the sick Mandans, and taking notes of all they saw and did kept the explorers busy during those dreary days. Sometimes only the blacksmith's busy hammer saved them from suffering hunger. The Indians would always give corn in return for the blacksmith's work. But day by day the deer and buffaloes became fewer, and finally almost disappeared. The hunters returned from their hunts empty-handed and exhausted. The Sioux sometimes annoyed them, and could not be punished. For some time corn was their only food, but fortunately they succeeded in getting enough of this to keep them alive.

In February they lifted their boats out of the frozen river, and drew them up on the banks to repair them and make them ready for further service.

In March, hope returned with the northward flight of ducks, swans, and geese. Spring was near at hand, and everybody in the camp was busy. New boats were built, deer-skin ropes were made, axes were fashioned, corn was shelled, and all their supplies and presents were put out to dry.

On the first of April rain fell for the first time in five and a half months. This softened and smoothed the river so much that they at once slipped their boats into the water. The provisions and party for the westward journey were stowed away in six small canoes and two pirogues. Thirty-two men turned their faces west, sixteen men turned their faces east. The latter were on board the old barge and were to return to St. Louis, carrying maps and messages and huge boxes of specimens for President Jefferson. Some of the things carried back were:

Some stuffed antelopes.	Tail of a deer.
One weasel.	Skins of various animals.
Three squirrels.	Indian dress.
Skeleton of a prairie wolf.	Indian bow and arrows.
A white and a gray hare.	Indian tobacco-seed.
Two burrowing squirrels.	Box of plants.
One white weasel.	Box of insects.
Horns of mountain ram.	Prairie hen.
Horns of an elk.	Four magpies.

CHAPTER XII

FIGHTS WITH GRIZZLY BEARS

For days the voyage up the river was un-
eventful. Every creek, island, bird, beast, fruit,
or flower was closely observed and faithfully described. The weather was generally fine, game
became more plentiful, and the Yellowstone River
was reached without adventure.

The greatest cause of discomfort to the explorers was the sand and dust. When people
nowadays cross the continent a certain part of
their journey is made very uncomfortable by the
alkali dust. Even in the vestibuled trains, with
double windows, deflectors, and screens, this dreadful dust sifts over everything and almost chokes
the traveler. Think how much worse it must
have been for these men. The dust was so thick
at times that they could not see from one bank of
the river to the other. Their eyes grew very sore.
Their food was covered with dust; the water was
full of it. But it was only one of many discomforts, forgotten as soon as it was past.

The party had now reached the stretch of country most thickly infested by all kinds of wild and savage beasts. Wolves, buffaloes, and bears were seen every day, and now and then a panther, or American tiger, was met with. One night the camp was asleep. Suddenly the guard heard a noise of galloping feet. A buffalo, dripping wet from his swim across the river, crashed over the canoes on the river's bank, plunged straight into the camp-fire, careered down a row of sleeping men within eighteen inches of their heads, ran between four fires, barely escaped the heads of another row of men, whirled about toward the tent, was stopped by a dog, and then plunged bellowing off into the darkness.

But the men cared nothing for a buffalo. The one animal they feared was the grizzly, or, as they called it, "white" bear. This bear the Indians feared too. In fact, the Indians' fear of it was so great that they never dared to attack it unless in parties. They prepared for the hunt of the grizzly just as they did for war. War paint was put on, and war ceremonies were performed.

And there was good reason for fear, for the grizzly bear is one of the most dreadful of beasts. Its skin is very tough, and sometimes as many as eight shots would strike one before it fell. To kill this animal the shot must be in the head or heart. Grizzly bears have been known to run a quarter of a mile with a shot through the heart before they fell dead.

A FAMILY OF GRIZZLIES

Again and again Captain Lewis had been chased by one of these fierce fellows. He almost always killed the bear, but only after a long battle. Late one evening, Captain Clark encountered and shot a huge grizzly. The bear fled with an awful roar. Ten times it was wounded, but even then the beast swam half-way across the river before it dropped dead on a sand bar.

At another time the men in the boats were startled at the sight of one of their companions on shore running toward the boats shouting and crying. A grizzly, which he had shot through the lungs, had given chase and followed him for half a mile. Captain Clark and seven men instantly started in pursuit. Two hours later the bear was found lying in a deep hole it had dug in its fury. Two shots in the head at last closed the battle.

A few days later the men in the canoes saw a huge bear lying on shore. Six hunters landed and attacked the beast. Four bullets struck him, two of them piercing his lungs. Maddened with pain, he whirled about and rushed at the hunters. Two of them fired and broke the bear's shoulder. Before they could reload, the bear was upon them. Two men jumped headlong into the canoes, while the other four hunters hid themselves, firing again and again. Still the bear came on. Flinging away guns, pouches, everything, the four men leaped down a twenty-foot bank and plunged into the river. The bear tore after, and had just grasped a man, when a shot from the shore struck the bear in the head and killed him. Eight wounds were found on his body. The men took the huge skin back to camp.

CHAPTER XIII

AN IMPORTANT DECISION

When the hunters reached the camp they found everything in confusion. One of the canoes loaded with the most valuable possessions of the party had been nearly capsized in a sudden squall. Three men had barely escaped with their lives. Medicines, instruments, and papers had been badly injured, but not entirely ruined. It was necessary that all the freight should be examined, dried, repaired, and then repacked. This caused a delay of some days.

It seemed as though the whole month of May was full of disaster and hard work. The mud was deep, the river almost impassable. A quarter of the time the men were up to their armpits in water, walking over rough rocks, dragging heavy canoes, and keeping everything in as good order as possible; still they uttered no word of complaint. Gradually the character of the country began to change; the rivers grew narrower and the current more rapid, the banks were less wooded and more broken. Hills and small mountains began to appear in the distance.

Late in May, Captain Lewis caught his first glimpse of the Rocky Mountains, "the object of all our hopes, and the reward of all our ambitions." Now the towlines of knotted elk-skin were brought into use, for the rapids were frequent and danger threatened the cargoes at every turn. The scenery grew more striking; the banks were in some places three hundred feet high, washed by the rains and colored in strange fashion.

Again the country fell away. Game reappeared. At the mouth of a large river of which they had not heard, the explorers encamped. They called this stream Marias River. Now they were face to face with a great problem.

Which river was the Missouri? Which river should they ascend? The success of the whole expedition depended upon this decision. If they ascended the wrong river, valuable time would be lost, and the men would be worn out and discouraged. In order to settle this question, two canoes and three men were sent up each river. These men were to measure the depth and rapidity of the stream, while others were sent by land to discover the general direction in which it flowed.

In the meantime Lewis and Clark climbed to the top of a high hill. Around them hopped, ran, and flew linnets, goldfinches, blackbirds, robins, and turtledoves. From the top of the hill could be seen great herds of buffaloes and antelopes, with prowling wolves following each herd.

For a little distance both rivers could be seen, while the mountains lay far beyond. The northern branch, or Marias River, was yellow and turbid, just as the Missouri had been all the way. The southern branch was clear, cold, and rapid, as if it came from the mountains. Moreover, the Indians had said the water at the falls of the Missouri was clear and sparkling. On the other hand, they had said nothing of this northern branch.

In the end the captains agreed that the clear, rapid stream must be the Missouri. The men did not think so, but cheerfully prepared to follow their leaders. For fear of error it was, however, arranged that Lewis and four men should travel by land along the southern branch until either the falls or the mountains were reached. The rest of the party was to follow more closely by water. One of the large boats was therefore drawn up on land and hidden, while their heavy baggage was placed in a cache.

CHAPTER XIV

MAKING A CACHE

Making a cache requires very hard and careful work. First, the men found a dry spot high above the river. On the grass they drew a small circle twenty inches across, and carefully lifted out the sod. A hole a foot deep was dug straight down and then widened out like a big kettle, six or seven feet deep. As fast as the dirt was loosened it was lifted up and out in some kind of a vessel and laid carefully on a cloth. Not a bit of dirt must be allowed to fall on the ground. This dirt was then carried away and dropped into the river. A floor of dry sticks was laid in the bottom of the kettle-like hole and some hay or a dry buffalo skin was spread over it. Then the baggage which they had dried and aired was laid upon the buffalo skin. Sticks were put about the baggage to keep it from touching the sides of the cache. A skin was spread over the things, earth was thrown down and packed hard, and the sod put back so perfectly that no one could see the least mark.

Two of these caches were made, while in two other places lead and powder were hidden, lest some accident might happen to the caches.

Lewis then set off with his four men. They killed all the game they could, and hung it up on the trees for the men who were following in the boats.

WILD TURKEYS

It was at this time that two bears were killed by the first bullets that struck them, a thing which happened only this one time. Deer and wild turkeys and other game were abundant. Everything was going happily, when Captain Lewis became seriously ill.

For a day or two he dragged painfully along. He grew no better. He had no medicine. At last he gathered some herbs, made a strong hot drink, and hastily swallowed it down. The next morning he was better, and his strong will carried him safely through. This was well, for a few days later he met with an adventure which required all the strength at his command.

CHAPTER XV

AN EXCITING MORNING

One morning as Captain Lewis was pushing rapidly along through the woods, he suddenly heard the distant muffled roar of falling water, and saw a cloud of spray like a column of smoke. Hurrying over the seven miles which lay between him and this smoke-like column, he was delighted to find that it was caused by the magnificent falls of the Missouri.

The falls, with their hundreds of feet of tumbling rapids, claimed his close attention for a few moments. But his chief interest lay in finding some way to pass the falls with his loaded boats, which would shortly arrive. A short walk brought into view another glorious fall, and still a little farther on a third appeared. Rapids, falls, cascades, in quick succession, greeted the explorer's delighted and impatient gaze. Even an eagle's nest which the Indians had spoken of in describing the falls was seen and recognized.

Climbing to the top of a hill, he saw the river

above the falls, calm and undisturbed, and still deep enough to carry the boats. A herd of a thousand buffaloes offered meat enough for his supper. He shot one, and stood with rifle unloaded

FALLS OF THE MISSOURI

waiting for the buffalo to fall. Suddenly, to his horror, he saw a huge bear not twenty steps away. With an unloaded rifle, he could only run for his life. Across the open plain he fled; no tree, no bush, no bank—and the bear, open-mouthed, was close behind him. Hope was almost gone when, thinking of the river, he turned, leaped into the water, and with clubbed gun faced the bear, which was only a few yards behind him. Frightened by Lewis's defiance, the great beast whirled and fled madly across the plain, and soon disappeared in the distance.

Wading out of the river and loading his rifle, Lewis quietly proceeded until he was startled by a panther which was crouching directly in his path. The animal being just ready to spring, Lewis was none too quick in sending him wounded into his hiding place among the rocks.

Only a few steps farther on three buffaloes, catching sight of him, left the herd and came plunging and bellowing toward him. Lewis walked straight toward them. When he was within three hundred feet of them they suddenly whirled and running back rejoined the herd.

The thorns of the prickly pear, which grew here abundantly and which were constantly piercing his feet, seemed to Captain Lewis the only proof that this land was not bewitched.

When finally he rejoined his men, they received him with great joy; for his long absence had alarmed them, and searching parties were just setting out to find him.

CHAPTER XVI

PASSING THE FALLS

While Captain Lewis was having these exciting adventures, the party coming by river was not altogether comfortable. The men were in the water much of the time, tugging at the unwieldy boats. Their feet were badly cut by rough stones, and often bitten by snakes, but their cheerful spirits never failed them. They knew they were moving straight ahead, and doing what they had set out to do.

At length Captain Clark and the boats arrived at the falls and rapids. It was very hard work to get the boats through any rough water; and the only way of passing the falls was by a portage with wagons. Six of the men were detailed to make a kind of truck for the boats and baggage. Choosing a huge cottonwood-tree they made the wheels. This was done by sawing off cross-sections of the tree where it was largest. They then took the mast of one of the boats for an axle. While wagons were being made the hunters were scouring the country for provisions. Some elks were killed and brought in, and the meat was jerked. Fish were caught. Berries were gathered and dried. But buffalo meat was still their main food. Between the narrow rock passages to the falls great droves of these animals came to drink. Those in front were crowded and pushed by those behind, so that sometimes several buffaloes would be shoved headlong into the seething falls, and go tumbling down the rapids. Extra provisions were cached near the falls. Captain Clark started ahead to drive stakes to mark the path which the rest were to follow. Maps and carefully drawn diagrams were made of the falls and rapids.

The awkward wagons were finally ready, and loaded with the baggage from the boats. Then the men laid hold of them and pulled and pushed with all their might. The great wheels creaked and groaned, and the whole party moved slowly forward toward the head of the falls. After going eight miles the wagon broke down. It was mended and slowly moved on again—helped now by the sails of the boats set to catch a favoring breeze. Half a mile from the head of the falls the wagon broke down again, and the men carried the baggage the remaining distance by hand. Clark had

kept well ahead, choosing the shortest and best
route for the portage. Some of the men were
limping dreadfully from the wounds of the prickly
pear and the rough ground; others were so ex-

PASSING
THE
FALLS

hausted they could
only stand a few
moments at a time.   At every halt men dropped
to the ground and instantly fell asleep.

At length the falls were passed, and a camp was
made above them.   Here the men set to work
to make a skin boat.   The iron frame had been
brought from Virginia.   When completed and the

seams calked with a preparation of mud, the boat was launched and loaded. Great was the delight of the explorers at its apparent success. Greater was their disappointment when the next morning the seams were open, and the boat was on the point of sinking. Again and again they tried to cure the trouble, but the seams would crack in spite of every effort. This was perhaps the keenest disappointment Captain Lewis had suffered in the whole journey. When thoroughly convinced that nothing could be done, the iron frame was hidden, and a canoe thirty-three feet long was made from the trunk of a large tree.

While still at this camp, Captain Clark, the Indian woman, her husband and child, and two or three of the men had a narrow escape from death. A heavy rain came sweeping down upon them from the mountains, and the narrow ravine was suddenly filled with a torrent which carried everything before it. Before Clark could snatch his gun and shot-bag, and push the Indian woman and child up the side of the bluff, the water reached his waist. The flood rose fifteen feet. An instant's hesitation and all would have been swept into the river and over the falls. The rest of the party, who on account of the heat and hard work wore but few clothes, were almost killed by the hail. Knocked down, bruised, and bleeding, they came painfully back to camp. These sudden storms of rain, hail, snow, or sleet often came sweeping down from the mountains carrying everything before them.

The portage being passed, the reunited party took time to make important observations, collect their baggage, and repair damages. Here they celebrated their second Fourth of July. They often heard curious noises in the mountains—like the firing of guns or like heavy explosions. These noises they could never account for.

At length the leaders carefully cached their maps and extra provisions and gathered the party for the most trying stage of the entire journey. The mountains towered above them. Over these mountains their path lay through unbroken forests and perhaps among unfriendly tribes of Indians.

Captain Clark and three men went ahead, in order to find the Indians before they should be frightened into their mountain hiding-places by the sound of the white man's gun. They were too late. The Indians had disappeared. Spreading a trail of cloth, paper, and linen, that the Indians might know they were white men, Clark plodded on by land, while Lewis directed the party coming by water. One day the Indian woman gave a grunt of joy. She had seen and recognized a great rock shaped like a buffalo's head and she knew she was in her own country.

Following Indian roads when they appeared, and making their own roads when they did not

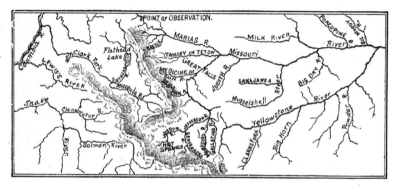

HEADWATERS OF THE MISSOURI AND THE COLUMBIA

appear, the party finally arrived at the three forks of the Missouri. They named one of these forks Madison, another Gallatin, and the third Jefferson.

Directed by a note from Captain Clark which they found stuck on a pole, the water party proceeded up the Jefferson River. They hoped to reach the headwaters of the Columbia, but before this could be done horses must be bought and the mountain ridge crossed.

CHAPTER XVII

UP THE JEFFERSON RIVER

At this point Captain Clark was taken ill. While waiting for his recovery the men put deer-skins to soak and prepared to make clothes of them. The thermometer stood at 90 degrees, and it seemed as if they could never need such clothes. But the snow-capped mountains above them were a warning.

In a few days the party moved on, much delighted and encouraged by the Indian woman's recognition of different places through the country. Here she saw the spot where she had been taken captive by the Knife Indians and carried down the river. There was the spot where a hunting-camp had been.

On account of Clark's illness, Lewis now scouted ahead. He suffered every discomfort and inconvenience—wading rivers, plunging through brushwood, sleeping anywhere, and often going hungry.

Captain Clark, meanwhile, brought on the

water party. The river grew so rough and the banks so steep and heavy with brushwood that the men were obliged to wade the river and drag the canoes.

Coming to the mouth of the Wisdom River, they were disappointed to find no note from Lewis. The pole on which it was stuck had been cut down by a beaver and the note lost.

Being without any clew, they unfortunately chose the wrong branch, and ascending the Wisdom River instead of the Jefferson, camped on an island for the night. The island was so low that they had to cut brushwood to lie upon. This kept them from lying in the water.

The next day they toiled onward until overtaken by a messenger, who told them of their mistake, and they retraced their way to the Jefferson River. A canoe was upset while returning, and many valuable things were lost. A man who was thrown from the canoe was badly bruised and with difficulty escaped drowning.

Indian guides and horses must now be found, and Lewis and some others slung their knapsacks over their shoulders, saying they should not be seen again until they had found these necessary things.

Leaving notes at the forks of the river for Clark and his party, Lewis pressed boldly onward. One can imagine his delight and that of his companions when, worn out and hungry, they saw in the distance a horseman. They knew that he belonged to a tribe not seen before. He was seated on a fine horse. The horse was without a saddle, and an elk-skin string fastened to its lower jaw served as a bridle. Lewis walked eagerly toward the Indian. When a mile away he took his blanket from his bag, held it by the two corners, and, unfolding it, spread it on the ground.

This is the sign of friendship among all Indian tribes on the Missouri River and through the Rocky Mountains. Three times Lewis did this—spreading the blanket in his most inviting manner.

But the Indian seemed afraid. Lewis walked slowly forward. He took from his bag some beads and trinkets. He dropped his gun, but at two hundred yards the Indian whirled and rode away. Lewis called out "tábba bone," which means "white man," but, still watching the advance of the two other men, the Indian rode away. Lewis spoke to his men. One heard and stopped, the other did not hear and did not stop. Again the

Indian halted, but at one hundred and fifty yards turned and rode hastily away.

More disappointed than he could express, Lewis made an attempt to follow him. Tying an American flag to a pole, the three men walked on. They built a fire, hoping to attract attention. They tied some trinkets on a pole, thinking they were near the Indian camp and the presents would be seen. Soon, however, a rain came up. This spoiled the trail of the horse in the grass, and, discouraged, they gave up the search.

The next morning Lewis and the two men encircled the mountain. They crossed several small streams and found places where the Indians had been digging roots. They also saw Indian trails, but they found no Indians.

Following one of these trails, they came to a tiny stream which they knew must be a source of the Missouri River. Astride of this stream one of the men said he "thanked God he had lived to put a foot on each side of the Missouri River!"

A source of the Missouri River never before seen by white men, a clear and icy stream, trickled at their feet. Down they sat, thinking themselves well repaid for all their labor. The end of the seemingly endless river had been discovered.

CHAPTER XVIII

THE COLUMBIA RIVER REACHED

As the explorers resumed their journey and pushed boldly onward over the mountains, they hoped that they might find the head of some little stream which, flowing westwardly, would prove this ridge of mountains to be the great dividing-line between the Missouri and the Columbia. Very soon this hope was realized. Within three quarters of a mile they came upon a fine clear stream running west.

Again they stopped. They drank for the first time of waters flowing toward the Pacific. A scrap of raw pork, their only remaining bit of food, made their supper; but little they cared for hunger when they could drink from the head waters of the Columbia!

A day or two later more Indians were sighted, but instantly disappeared. Their dogs, however, followed the explorers until Lewis tried to tie some trinkets about their necks; then they slunk quickly away.

Before night three Indian women were seen. One of them ran away; the other two dropped to the ground and hung their heads. They expected instant death. Lewis lifted them up, and stripping up his sleeve showed them his white skin; for his face and hands were as brown as any Indian's. He then proved himself a friend by giving them some presents, and the women at once guided him to their camp.

On their way they were met by sixty warriors riding at full speed. Lewis dropped his gun, put up his little American flag, and walked gravely toward them. The women told their story. At once three of the leaders sprang from their horses, threw their right arms over Lewis's left shoulder, clasped his back, laid their left cheeks to his, and said "Ah-hi-e" over and over. This meant they were "pleased to meet him." All the warriors saluted the brave captain in the same way, leaving him decidedly greasy and much stained with war paint.

Lewis then lighted a pipe, and offered it to the Indians. Before they accepted it, however, they pulled off their moccasins, which was their way of saying that they would go barefooted all their lives in order to prove themselves his friends.

INDIANS FISHING FOR SALMON

White men and red then went on together to the Indian camp.

Young braves hurried ahead and prepared a tent for Captain Lewis. Boughs and skins were spread on the floor, except in the middle of the tent. Here the grass was pulled up, and preparations were made for the same kind of ceremony we read of a little while ago. This being over, presents were given to the women and children.

Lewis then told the Indians that his men had eaten nothing since the day before. The chief replied that they themselves had nothing but some cakes made of dried berries. These they gladly gave, and the white men as gladly ate. A walk to the small stream followed this poor meal. The Indians said that the stream soon became wider, but that there was no wood on its banks large enough for canoes.

On the way back to the camp a young Indian called Lewis into his tent and gave him a bit of smoked salmon. This was proof indeed that they were on the Columbia River. No other river produced such fish as that, but Lewis did not know it. A dance closed this exciting day, but long before the harsh music died away Lewis had withdrawn to his own tent.

CHAPTER XIX

AMONG THE INDIANS

Among these friendly mountain people Lewis decided to stay, and wait for Captain Clark and the remainder of the party. He had nothing but parched corn and dried berries for food. Every moment was spent in studying the country and the people, and in planning the details for the remaining part of the journey. No game but antelopes could be found, and these could seldom be caught. The Indian manner of hunting them was most interesting to watch, but rather disappointing in its results. The hunters would place themselves in groups about a great circle. In the middle of the circle was the herd of antelopes. One group of hunters would then rush out on their trained ponies and chase the herd across the plain to another group of hunters. These hunters would chase them back. Another set would then rush out from another point and take up the hunt. This was kept up until the game was worn out, or could be reached by the hunters' arrows. Often all escaped, and the men would return with foaming horses, but no game. Forty or fifty hunters would sometimes work all day for two or three antelopes.

Finding the Indians continued to be friendly, Lewis tried to persuade them to send a party of men and horses with him to meet Captain Clark. After many trials they finally promised, but again and again they put off the start. They feared that Lewis was trying to deceive them, and that the party would prove to be enemies. At last Lewis made a long and wise speech, in which he asked them if they were afraid. Now this is a tender point with an Indian. He will face any danger rather than be thought cowardly. As a result the chief said he at least would go, if he went alone. A small party joined him, and they set out, leaving their squaws lamenting loudly. The squaws believed their braves were riding to certain death. The party had not gone far when more braves joined them, and though they felt very suspicious, they really did stay with Lewis until he met Clark.

I have said that the explorers had little to eat, Lewis himself often going hungry. One day a deer was killed. The Indians greedily ate the intestines as fast as the hunters threw them aside. They did not touch the good meat, however, until it was given to them, but when it was given to them they ate it raw.

Now, although Lewis had said he would meet his party at the forks of the river, he knew they might be delayed. If they were not there the Indians would instantly kill him. So he sent one of his men with one of the Indians and told him to bring a note which he would find stuck in a pole at the forks. This was his own note, written and left for Captain Clark. By telling the Indians it had been put on the pole for him by a messenger from Clark's party, he succeeded in keeping them quiet. He said the note told him they were delayed, but would soon arrive. He then sent another messenger down the river to hurry Clark along if he should meet him.

It was a very anxious time, but Lewis was cheerful and apparently careless, and his courage was soon rewarded by the sight of the party. The Indians showed their own relief by embracing Lewis fervently.

While they were waiting, Lewis had told them of the Indian woman of their own tribe, Sacajawea, and the black man, York. When she, sitting in one of the boats, saw the party, she began to dance, to sing, and give every sign of great joy. She sucked her fingers to let them know that she belonged to their tribe. When the savages saw her they shouted joyfully, and when they drew nearer, some of them recognized her as an old acquaintance. They greeted her in their boisterous way, and welcomed her back to her own people and country.

At once Lewis was seated on a white robe, and the chief tied six small white shells in his hair. This was a mark of great honor. Moccasins were taken off and the peace-pipe smoked. Then Sacajawea was called in to act as interpreter. Just as she was beginning to talk she suddenly stopped; then she jumped up,

SACAJAWEA
THE INTERPRETER'S WIFE

flung her arms about one of the braves, threw her blanket over him, and burst out crying. The young man was her brother. From him she learned that her entire family was dead, except two brothers and a small nephew. This boy she at once took for her own. –

CHAPTER XX

HESITATION

When the woman was quiet enough to act as interpreter, speeches were made explaining the purpose of the expedition, and asking the Indians if they would help them by selling them some horses. The Indians replied that they would do all they could, They said the party could not travel by water because of the rapids in the river.

One Indian drew a map, using a stick for a pencil and the dust for paper. He showed where the river ran, and made little piles of sand for the mountains. He said these mountains were covered with snow, and that the banks of the river were solid rock. The river itself was covered with foam. He declared no nation had ever crossed these mountains, but they had all heard of a river running to an ill-tasting lake.

Other Indians told him they would have steep mountains to cross where there was no game. There would be roots to eat, but they would have to fight for them with the mountain Indians, who lived like bears in holes. They said the horses' feet would be cut to pieces by the rough road.

After a time they would come to a desert, where for ten days they would find no grass nor water for horses. They must then pass through many hostile tribes, but if they kept on they would at last reach the ocean. One man promised to go with them if they would wait until spring. Lewis and Clark both felt that this route through the desert would lead them to the Gulf of California, and not to Oregon. So they chose a more northerly route, and Clark set out with eleven men to see whether the trip must really be by land instead of water.

Lewis remained with the friendly Indians, and bought some horses. He paid queer prices for them. He bought three good horses for a coat, some leggings, handkerchiefs, and knives; in value to him about twenty dollars, but wealth to the Indians. Later the price rose, and a horse cost a pistol, a knife, and a hundred rounds of powder and ball.

As Clark and his men pursued their journey they were provided with salmon, dried and fresh, which the Indians caught in weirs. The way proved as difficult as the Indians had said. Salmon were scarce, the Indians were leaving the river for their winter hunting-grounds, and Clark was convinced that travel by water was impossible. He therefore retraced his steps and tried another route; and though he fell and severely hurt his knee, still he pushed on.

Again convinced of the uselessness of such attempts, Clark sent a messenger to Lewis with his decision. With no food but berries, which made them all ill, and sometimes without any food at all, they hurried to meet Lewis.

With wasting strength, they encamped and decided to go no farther, but to wait there for the coming of Lewis and his party. They cached all extra baggage, and when Lewis joined them, nine days later, preparations for the mountain journey were well advanced.

Lewis had secured twenty-nine horses from the Shoshones, whose wealth was horses. But he also had suffered much from lack of food and threatened treachery. Once he had proved his sincerity by giving the whole of a deer to the women and children of the tribe while going hungry himself.

The Indians from whom Lewis had gotten the horses had many interesting customs and ceremonies. One of these ceremonies was the making of a shield. When some warrior needed a shield, a feast was given to all the old men, warriors, and jugglers. After the feast a hole eighteen inches deep was dug in the ground. This hole was the same size as the shield they wished to make. Red-hot stones were then thrown into the hole, and water poured over the stones. Of course a heavy steam would rise. Then the entire fresh hide of a buffalo was laid across the hole, the fleshy side down, and everybody took hold of it and stretched it with all their might. When they thought it had been stretched enough, they set to work and pounded it with their bare heels as hard as they could pound. This pounding would last several days. The shield was then declared proof against arrows or bullets, and handed over to the owner.

They always fought on horseback; and they had armor for themselves and their horses, made of layers and layers of the skins of antelopes. They made fire by whirling one stick around on another, and, like many tribes, they cut their hair as a sign of mourning. They used very few metal tools, and had only a few knives, brass kettles, bracelets, buttons, and spearheads, which they had gained by trading. In spite of all their warlike characteristics they were kind to the aged.

CHAPTER XXI

DOWN THE SNAKE RIVER

But the time came when our party must move on, and the month which followed was full of dreadful experiences. Rain, snow, hail, and sleet impeded their way. Bushes had to be cut down and fallen trees climbed over.

The horses sometimes slipped and fell long distances down the sides of the mountain. Sometimes they strayed away in the night. One horse loaded with a desk and a small trunk rolled over, and over for a hundred and twenty feet and then bumped against a great tree, which stopped him. The desk was broken, but the horse was not hurt at all. Two horses dropped exhausted and had to be left behind, while the men took up their loads. More horses had to be bought from tribes in the mountains.

The men were often wet to the skin and suffered from frozen feet. There were streams to cross and recross full of ice and water. The baggage was frozen. Much time was lost in trying to get food. At last it became necessary to kill a colt for food, and the creek where they were then camped was called "Colt Killed Creek."

The men grew low-spirited. No game could be found. A second colt was killed, and a third; and one night there was nothing to eat but a little canned soup. The creek where they encamped that night they called "Hungry Creek."

Occasionally Indian tribes were met, and though they had but little food, they gladly shared it. Even this amount of food after their long hunger made many of the men ill, and when a few days later roots became plentiful, all the men were very sick from overeating.

Late in September they came to navigable water, and found trees large enough for making canoes. The horses were collected and branded, and given into the care of the Indians to be kept until the return of the explorers.

Saddles were cached, as well as powder and balls. The canoes were finished and launched, and once more the explorers were floating down a river. It was not smooth sailing, however, for rocks were plentiful, and the upsetting of a boat was a common occurrence.

At last the present site of Lewiston, Idaho, was

reached. There the Indians fairly swarmed about them, and from them the explorers bought a few dogs for change of diet. These Indians made fun of them and called them "dog-eaters." They were of the Chopunnish tribes that never ate dog.

Down the Snake River they floated, buying dogs and fish, and driving sharp bargains with the natives. Among these Indians they noted one curious custom, most uncommon among savages. They took baths! A hole was dug in the ground and covered closely, leaving room for several people inside. The bath was a social affair, and a refusal to bathe was a great insult. When the bathers were ready, they would go into the hole with a number of hot stones and jugs of water. The water was thrown on the stones and made a hot steam. In this steam the bathers sat for some time. Then, running out, they would leap into a cold stream, afterward going back to the steaming again.

In each tribe there were some interesting things to observe. The Sohulks were kind to old people, which was most unusual. Their wives were treated well, too, which was also unusual. But as a tribe they suffered from two great inconveniences. They had poor teeth and poor eyes.

CHAPTER XXII

DOWN THE COLUMBIA

At last the Columbia River was reached, and for a little time traveling proved more comfortable. Frequent councils were held, and the Indians were often entertained by being shown the wonders of the shotgun and burning-glass.

Lewis and Clark, on the other hand, were equally interested in seeing how the Indians prepared the famous Columbia River salmon. After the fish were caught they were dried in the sun, and pounded between two stones. Baskets made of rushes and grass, and lined with fish-skins, were then filled with the pounded fish, covered, and left outdoors until sold. The fish so prepared will keep good for years.

The Indian method of burying trout was also interesting. First a hole was dug and lined with straw. Over the straw skins were laid, and the trout put into the skins. Other skins were thrown over the fish, and the hole closed with dirt twelve or fifteen inches deep.

L. of C.

Late in October they caught their first glimpse of Mt. Hood, and within a few hours they arrived at the rapids above the falls of the Columbia. Whenever it could possibly be done, the canoes were let down by ropes, still keeping them in the water; but when the rocks were too thick and the current too rapid, there was nothing left to do but to carry the canoes overland.

Once past the falls, they saw what they had not seen since leaving the Indians in Illinois. These were wooden houses. They were very queerly built. First a large hole six feet deep, thirty feet long, and twenty feet wide was dug in the ground. This hole was then lined with boards, which reached just above the surface of the ground.

A roof was put on, a crack being left the whole length of the roof for the smoke to escape. A doorway twenty-nine and one-half inches high, fourteen inches wide, and eighteen inches above ground was left. In front of this a mat was hung for a door. Half of this house was used for storing fish and berries; the other half was used by the family. Little bedsteads were built around the sides, while the fire burned in the middle.

In a short time the explorers came to the rapids and narrows of the Columbia, now known

INDIANS ON HORSEBACK

as the Dalles. As the canoes were too large to be carried, and too heavily loaded to float in such shallow water, there was but one plan to follow, the baggage must be transferred by land, and the canoes let down by water. Accordingly the perilous descent began, watched by a great crowd of Indians. Three canoes slipped safely through the boiling water; the fourth was nearly filled with it, while the fifth escaped with but little damage. For half a mile the struggle was tremendous; two and a half miles more were hard, but after this the river broadened and became calm, and the boats dropped quietly down to the next rapids. Here it became necessary to slip some of the heavier canoes from one rock to another on poles, while the lighter ones were safely guided between them.

The Indian guides were sent back. The explorers needed them no longer. Tide water lapped the sides of their canoes.

As the explorers approached the mouth of the river, heavy fogs often hid the banks completely from their view, and made navigation dangerous. But one day in November the fog lifted, and the "ocean was in view! Oh, the joy! The object of all our labors ; the reward of all our anxieties."

The roar of the breakers was delightful music to the men, and "great cheerfulness" became the mood of the whole party. But the waves ran high, and the men became seasick. The water was too salty to use. The baggage could not be placed above the reach of the tide. At length they contrived to lift it on poles, and then "passed a disagreeable night." The rain fell dismally, the canoes were filled with water, the tide came booming in. Huge trees floating out with the current knocked against their camp, and the canoes were nearly crushed to pieces. All the next day was spent in the pouring rain, with only fish to eat and rainwater to drink. Still the men were cheerful.

On the following night the camp was made on driftwood by the shore. The tide rose high, and threatened to cover them. Stones came rolling down upon them from the cliffs above. The men, adrift on floating logs or hidden in the crevices of the rocks, cowered from the storm. The underbrush was so thick there was no escape by land. The hunters could not go out. Dry raw fish was their only food. The furious gale blew continuously. In despair Captain Clark pulled himself up the mountain-like cliff by bushes to reconnoiter, but clouds shut off his view.

CHAPTER XXIII

FORT CLATSOP AND THE START HOME

At the end of six days the storm subsided, and the men once more embarked. At the mouth of the Columbia they determined to make a permanent camp. They built some rough huts or cabins, called the place Fort Clatsop, and there lived four months, during which time the rain fell almost constantly. Food was hard to find, their clothing was in a deplorable condition, and they were obliged to pay outrageous prices to the Indians for anything they bought. Yet they did not despair.

Early in December Clark chronicled their arrival on the Pacific coast in these words which he cut into a tree: "William Clark, December 3, 1805. By land from the U. S. in 1804 and 5."

Christmas was celebrated as usual by a discharge of firearms and a song from the men. Handkerchiefs and tobacco were distributed as gifts and a dinner of spoiled elk's meat, a few roots, and some sour pounded fish was eaten with as good a grace as possible.

As soon as they could be spared, five men were sent to the sea, each armed with a kettle. In these kettles they were to boil sea-water and make some salt. Other men were sent out to hunt, while a third division was set to work making pickets and setting them up around the fort.

One day word was brought to the fort that a whale had drifted ashore at a point many miles distant. An eager party at once set out to see it. At times traveling in canoes, again climbing mountains, and enduring many discomforts, they pushed boldly forward toward the place that had been named. They met fourteen Indians loaded with oil and blubber. Then descending from the mountains and traversing the sandy beach for a long distance, they found the whale. Nothing remained but the skeleton, one hundred and five feet long. The Indians had stripped it and were busily boiling the blubber in a square wooden trough. Into this trough they dropped hot stones. When the oil was ready it was put into the bladder and intestines of the whale for preservation. A high price was paid for a very little blubber and oil, and the party returned to Fort Clatsop.

Thus the dreary months of winter wore away. The men were often ill, and longed for the return

journey to begin.   Feeling that they had accomplished all they could at Fort Clatsop, they only
waited a cessation of rain to start for home.

With difficulty they persuaded an Indian to
sell them a canoe for a coat and a bit of tobacco.
They had a second canoe which they had taken
from the Indians by way of reprisal for some elk
meat which the savages had stolen from them in
the winter.   It was leaky, however, and scarcely
seaworthy in the smoothest water.   Having calked
the seams in this canoe, they loaded both with
such poor baggage as they had, and then bidding
good by to Fort Clatsop, started, some by water,
some by land, upon their long journey homeward.

This was on the twenty-third of March, 1806.
That night they camped at the mouth of a small
creek only sixteen miles above Fort Clatsop. The
next day they bought a dog to serve as food for
the sick men, and then resumed their journey.

The passage up the river was slow and beset
with difficulties.   They tried to buy food from the
Indians, who either refused to sell or charged such
prices as could not be paid.   At length the hunters
brought in a little seal meat, three eagles, and a
large goose.   One day seven deer were shot, but
before they could be brought in the vultures had

picked them to the bone. There was much game, but the great ferns which grew on the river banks were so dry that the rustling noise made by the men pushing through them often frightened the animals away.

Thus during the first half of the month of April the explorers toiled slowly up the great river. Sometimes they would make a brief stop in some Indian settlement, partly for the purpose of trading and partly to observe and take note of the peculiar character and habits of these savage denizens of the woods. Sometimes the greater part of a day was spent in curing meat or in providing a store of such other food as could be obtained from the natives.

A potato-like root called wappato was much prized by the Indians, and at certain seasons of the year was their chief food. It was found in ponds, the plants growing up like water lilies from the mud at the bottom. It was gathered usually by the women. Each woman went out in her own canoe; and when she arrived at the proper place she would leap out into the water, which was sometimes almost shoulder high. There she would stand with her feet in the mud, and by means of her toes separate the bulb-like roots from the plants. The roots would then rise to the surface and the woman would throw them into the canoe.

On the eighteenth of April the explorers

THE DALLES OF THE COLUMBIA

reached the Dalles of the Columbia. You will remember the great difficulties which they encountered here on their downward journey; it is not surprising to learn that the ascent of the long rapids was much more laborious and dangerous than the descent had been.

CHAPTER XXIV

ASCENT OF THE COLUMBIA

It was found impossible to carry the canoes around the rapids, and they were therefore of no further use. Earnest efforts were made to trade them for horses, but with no success. When, however, the men began to split them to pieces, rather than leave them to the Indians, the savages relented and handed over some beads, which Lewis and Clark were very glad to get.

After leaving the falls, a forced march of several days brought the explorers to the tribe of the Walla Wallas. The welcome given by these good Indians seemed most refreshing to the captains. The chief himself stalked off to gather an armful of wood and bring them some fish. He urged them to remain and collect a supply of food.

When the savages learned the real intentions and plans of the explorers, they made every effort to help them. They told them of a road which would shorten their hard journey by eighty miles, and sold them a number of dogs. The chief brought a fine horse. For this he asked a kettle, but as there were no kettles · left, Clark gave him his own sword and some ammunition. This pleased the chief so much that the long-suffering party was treated to a dance in the evening.

At length the Columbia was left behind, and the expedition pushed eastward overland, along the Kooskooskee River. The Indians who lived in this region would not eat dogs, and made much fun of the "dog-eating men." One day when our men were dining, an Indian flung a live puppy into Lewis's plate. Lewis instantly threw it back, striking the Indian full in the face, and promised to follow the puppy with a tomahawk if such a thing happened again.

The reputation of the captains for curing sickness had preceded them, and was now of great use to them.

Early in May the Kooskooskee was crossed. On the same day the captains were surprised by an Indian bringing them two canisters of powder. These he said his dog had dug up. Lewis and Clark knew they were canisters which they had cached on the way down the river. They therefore went to see if the dogs had dug up the saddles cached near the same spot. Sure enough, the cache had been opened, but the old chief said the river had risen and done the mischief. He had reburied everything he could find.

They next tried to find the horses which they had left there. The chief had promised to take care of them for some guns and ammunition. A thoroughgoing search was undertaken, and a few of the horses were found. Some were in good condition, but others showed signs of hard usage.

The Indians were now gathering moss from the trees and cones from the pine trees. These they cooked and ate a little later in the season. Just now they had a few roots and some dried trout, which they generously shared with our men, and even gave them two fat horses. This generous gift was heartily appreciated by the explorers.

Lewis and Clark did their best to show their gratitude by curing the sick. In this work Clark seemed to be the favorite. Indeed, he seemed always to win the love and confidence of the Indians. While he gave out the medicine, Lewis conducted councils. He at last induced the Indians to promise guides to conduct them over the mountains. But the party must wait a month. As there seemed no help for it, they finally encamped in a place advised by the Indians.

CHAPTER XXV

CROSSING THE BITTER ROOT MOUNTAINS

This place had once been a village, but only a sunken circle now remained to mark the spot. Into this depression the men put their baggage, and around its edges they built their tents of grass and sticks. The camp was on the east side of the Kooskooskee River, and because it was in the country of the Chopunnish Indians, was called Camp Chopunnish. Good pasturage for the horses was near and the salmon were daily expected in the river.

No sooner were the explorers settled than a dozen Indians appeared on the opposite bank and began to sing. This was their sign of friendship, and their friendship was very genuine. They showed it by supplying them with more horses and by teaching them new ways of hunting and cooking game.

One day the hunters brought in some bear's meat, and the Indians cooked it in this queer way: First they built a hot fire and laid some smooth stones on it. The hot stones were laid side by side and covered with pine branches. The bear meat was then spread on the pine branches, and another layer of pine put over it. On top of this was placed another layer of meat and another layer of pine. Over this water was poured, and a layer of earth several inches deep covered the whole mass. Three hours later the "bake" was uncovered.

CHOPUNNISH DWELLINGS

The meat was very tender, but the taste of the pine spoiled it for the white men.

The principal game here was deer, and they were scarce. The Indians had a peculiar method of hunting them. A hunter would take a deer's head and skin, kept in shape by a frame of sticks, and holding it so it would look like a feeding deer, decoy the herd within reach of his arrows.

Meanwhile the days passed slowly, and at length about the middle of June the party left Camp Cho-

punnish, where they had been nearly a month, and
set out to cross the Bitter Root Mountains.

For twenty-two miles they struggled along
through slippery mud in a heavy rain. As they
got higher up on the mountains snow began to
appear. Soon they were traveling over drifts.
fifteen feet deep, with a crust hard enough to
bear the horses. The weather was so cold as to
benumb hands and feet, and make the danger of
freezing a constant one. At length they halted.
Should they go on or should they return? Travel
over the smooth, crusty snow was far easier than
through an unbroken wilderness where there was
not so much as a path. But on the other hand,
where there was snow there was no grass for the
horses.

After much deliberation it was decided to
leave the baggage, and, while the horses were still
strong, return where they could get food and
guides. Poles were put up between trees, and
the baggage, after being carefully covered with
skins, was hung from the poles. As this baggage
consisted largely of maps, papers, and instruments,
they felt it would be better to leave it than be
encumbered with it on the backward journey.

In all their thousands of miles of travel, this

was the first time they had ever been obliged to turn back because they could not overcome difficulties ahead. They had gone in the wrong direction and been forced to return once before, but that was only because a mistake had been made. The captains feared the men would be discouraged, but they were not; they knew it was necessary, and that was enough.

In a few days, finding the snow was not so deep around the trees, expert woodsmen were sent ahead to see if they could follow the trail. They were to examine the trees carefully. If they found marks made by the scraping of passing Indian ponies, they were to blaze these trees with tomahawks. The party could then easily follow the blazed trees.

Guides were secured, and the party started to make a second attempt to cross the Bitter Root Mountains. The top was safely reached. There they found the cache that had previously been made. The baggage was repacked, and the party hurried forward on top of ten feet of snow. The marks on the trees were very faint, but the guides went straight ahead without an instant's hesitation. Occasionally a bare spot of ground was seen, and the well-defined summer road it disclosed was proof that they were on the right trail. On they pushed day after day, and on the first of July they arrived on the banks of Clark's Fork at the mouth of a creek, which they called Travelers' Rest.

Here they decided to stay and rest a day or two, and then divide the expedition into two parties. Lewis with nine men was to go direct to the falls of the Missouri. Leaving three men there to make wagons to carry baggage and canoes around the falls, he with the other six men was to explore the Marias River.

The rest of the party under Clark was to go across country to that point on the Jefferson River where the explorers had cached their canoes and other articles on their way out. Sergeant Ordway with nine men was then to take these canoes and descend the river to its junction with the Missouri, and thence float down to the falls. The others with Captain Clark were to cross the open country to the Yellowstone River. There they were to build canoes, descend the river, and wait for Lewis at the junction of that stream with the Missouri.

We will first follow Captain Lewis and his men, and then the party of Captain Clark.

CHAPTER XXVI

CAPTAIN LEWIS'S ADVENTURES

Captain Lewis's Indian guides left him as soon as the trail became well defined and returned to their tribes.

Plains, woods, hills, rivers, and creeks were crossed. Early in July Lewis and his party arrived at a narrow pass through the mountains. To their great delight this pass proved to be through the dividing-ridge between the Columbia River and the Missouri River. It has ever since been known as Lewis and Clark's Pass.

About the middle of July they came to the cache which they had made nearly a year before at the head of the falls of the Missouri. To their great disappointment they found that a flood had soaked everything. Specimens of plants were ruined, but some maps and charts were uninjured. Nothing had happened to the cottonwood wagon-wheels, and the iron boat-frame was not hurt by its long burial.

The contents of one cache being examined, a

man was sent off to examine the other one. On the way he had a dreadful experience. Riding quietly along, he suddenly found himself within ten feet of a huge grizzly bear. His terrified horse whirled about and threw the man headlong under the bear's head. Lifting himself on his

INDIANS HUNTING BUFFALOES AT THE GREAT FALLS

hind feet, the great beast spread his forelegs for the hug which would have killed the man. Like a flash the man struck him with the butt-end of his gun. He broke the gun but knocked the bear to the ground. Scrambling up a tree, the man was out of reach before the bear could recover himself. But Mr. Bear quietly sat down under the branches and, licking his chops, waited for his

game to come down.   There he sat all the afternoon, but as night came on he lumbered slowly
away.   When he was well out of sight, the man
came down, and hastened back to the camp.

Ever since emerging from the pass they had
found food very plentiful.   Near the falls herds of
buffaloes, ten thousand strong, were seen.   Fat
dogs, pounded fish, tough roots, and boiled moss
were now things of the past.   The bellowing of the
buffaloes was so deafening that on some nights it
was difficult to sleep.   The horses, coming from
the land of no buffaloes, were much terrified, and
snorted and plunged with fright.

With his arrival at the falls of the Missouri,
the first part of Lewis's journey was accomplished.
He therefore, with three men, set out on horseback for the Marias River, and ascended it to one
of its sources.   At first thought this would seem
to be a useless journey, but it was thought necessary in order to settle the question whether its
entire course was in territory belonging to the
United States.

The other six men were left at the falls to
await the coming of Sergeant Ordway with his
party, when they would assist him in carrying the
canoes and baggage over the portage.   After this

they were to embark on the Missouri, and the parties were to reunite at the mouth of the Marias.

One day as Captain Lewis and his party were riding along the bank of the Marias River, they descried a band of about thirty Indians on horseback, hovering in the distance. Some of the Indian horses had saddles, and this led Lewis to suspect the party was a band of Minnetarees, who were great thieves. There was no way to retreat. There was nothing to do but to face the danger boldly. Hoisting the American flag, Captain Lewis and his men rode slowly forward.

The Indians were evidently watching one of Lewis's scouts who had been sent ahead, and when they caught sight of the other three men they fled in every direction. In a little while they cautiously returned and held a hurried consultation. Suddenly the chief left his comrades and rode straight toward Captain Lewis. Pulling his pony to a sudden halt one hundred steps from where Lewis stood, he coolly surveyed him for a moment, wheeled and rode back like the wind. In a few moments the entire band rode toward our party. Feeling that he would rather die than lose his maps, papers, and journals, Captain Lewis charged his men to resist to the last moment.

But the Indians when they arrived dismounted from their horses, shook hands with the white men, and asked to smoke with them. The pipe was produced, and presents were handed around. General good feeling prevailed, the danger seemed past, and both parties went into camp. There were many things to be discussed. Each party told the other its history and plans, and the smoking continued until about eleven o'clock.

Captain Lewis lay down to sleep. The dusky visitors appeared also to sleep. The fire crackled and burned low. The guard kept his silent watch. At daybreak all was quiet. A few moments later, as one of the men stood by the fire, an Indian slipped up behind him and snatched two guns. Two other Indians quickly secured the rifles of men still asleep. The alarm rang out, chase was given to the thieves, the rifles were recovered, and one Indian lay dead not fifteen steps away. The real reason for the snatching of the guns was soon discovered. It was a ruse. The main party of the Indians was driving off the horses. Seeing themselves hotly pursued, the Indians retreated in great haste. They succeeded in driving away only one of Captain Lewis's horses, while they left four of their own behind.

Fearing that this was only the beginning of trouble, and expecting another attack at the mouth of the Marias River, Captain Lewis attempted to reach that point first, and prepare for the combat. As the four men approached the place where the Marias joins the Missouri, shots were heard. They hurried forward, but to their "exquisite satisfaction" they saw, instead of Indians, the six men who had been left at the Great Falls, and also Sergeant Ordway's party of nine, who had joined them a few days before. To Captain Lewis this fortunate meeting seemed almost too good to be true.

Rain, rain, rain followed for several days. Hurrying down the Missouri River, Captain Lewis and his little party passed the Big Dry, the Milk, the Porcupine, and many smaller branches of that great river. The current was rapid, the boatmen were of the best, and their progress was unhindered by any adverse circumstances. On the 17th of August they reached the Yellowstone. Here they had hoped to find Clark's party, but instead they found only a note which informed them that the party had been there, but had moved on.

Captain Lewis, therefore, again embarked, and floated swiftly down the stream, hoping to reach Captain Clark's camp in the night. In this, however, he was disappointed. With the dawn of the next day he gave up the chase, and proceeded in a more leisurely manner.

On the 11th a large herd of elks was seen on a sand bar that was thickly over- grown with wil- lows. Captain Lewis with one of the hunters went on shore to shoot some of them. Dressed in his brown elk-skin suit, he was cau- tiously approach- ing the herd when, through the care- lessness of the

AMERICAN ELKS

other hunter, he received a severe gunshot wound in the thigh. The wound was dressed, and the men, again embarking, floated rapidly down the stream.

The very next day Captain Clark's party was overtaken at a point a little below the mouth of Little Knife Creek. So ended the exploration of Captain Lewis's party.

CHAPTER XXVII

CAPTAIN CLARK'S ADVENTURES

In the meantime what had Captain Clark been doing?

You will remember he had left Captain Lewis at the junction of Travelers' Rest Creek with Clark's Fork, and that he had started up this river in a southerly direction with fifteen men and fifty horses. His company celebrated July 4th by an early halt and a feast of roots and a small piece of venison. For several days thereafter they pushed steadily forward, fording numerous streams, coming occasionally upon deserted campfires, and following the tracks of buffalo herds, bearing always in mind the chief object of their expedition, to learn all that they could about the geography of that remarkable region.

Retarded by rains, they were a long time in reaching the cache on the Jefferson River. They traveled a hundred and sixty-four miles through a mountain pass, where if the trees were only cut down a road good enough for wagons could be made.   The discovery of this easy pass proved afterward to be of great importance, although Captain Clark did not realize it at the time.

The canoes which had been left at the cache were now launched on the river, and the party proceeded, some by land and others by water. Those in the canoes took care of the baggage, while Clark and the men on shore examined the country.   The party on the water proceeded more rapidly, however, than the men on land, and Clark decided to join the former.   Both parties reached the junction of the Jefferson and the Gallatin at almost the same hour.   Sergeant Ordway and nine men now embarked in a canoe, intending to float down the Missouri to the great falls. We have already seen that he did this and afterward joined Lewis at the mouth of the Marias.

Sacajawea, the squaw, acted as guide to Captain Clark's party, and following her directions they safely reached the high land which divides the headwaters of the Yellowstone River from those of the Missouri.   Nine miles beyond this they arrived at the Yellowstone, just below the place where it issues from the mountains.   A bold and rapid stream it was, a hundred and twenty yards broad, and widening to nearly two miles in the valley below.

Since they could find no trees large enough to make canoes, it was necessary to continue the journey on horseback. This was a hard task, for the horses' feet were worn almost to the quick. If they had not been fitted with buffalo-skin moccasins, they would soon have been unable to walk.

At a distance of eighteen miles down the river Captain Clark found a fine grove in which were several trees large enough for small canoes. Here a camp was made, and the entire company settled down for a few days' hard work. Some were engaged in making canoes, others in hunting or in dressing skins for clothing. At the end of the fourth day two canoes, each twenty-eight feet long, eighteen inches deep, and about twenty-four inches wide, had been made. These canoes were lashed together and packed with baggage, and when everything was in readiness the company embarked and the journey was resumed.

Occasionally interesting Indian signs were seen. One day a lodge decorated with eagles' feathers and circular bits of wood, a bush of cedar and a buffalo head, was discovered. Another day a huge rock was seen curiously carved by the Indians. Clark named this rock Pompey's Pillar, and cut his own name upon it. His name may still be seen there.   From this rock the view was a wide one.   There were mountains, deep valleys, winding rivers, and high cliffs, and on the plains were grazing herds of elks and buffaloes.

On the 27th of July they took their last look at the Rocky Mountains, which had been constantly in sight since the 1st of May.   On the 3d of August they reached the mouth of the Yellowstone, and encamped on the same spot where they had stopped on their way up more than fifteen months before.   Here the canoes were unloaded, and the baggage spread out to dry.

As a result of this expedition, Captain Clark learned that the Yellowstone River is navigable for nearly nine hundred miles.   At its mouth was a fine place for a trading post or fort.   Only a few years later such buildings were actually erected. At this commanding spot the mosquitoes were found to be in full possession, and Captain Clark was forced, much against his will, to move on. He accordingly re-embarked, and the canoes, with his whole company on board, dropped slowly down the river.   On the 12th of August, to the great joy of all, they were overtaken by Captain Lewis's party.   The explorers were once more united in a single party.

CHAPTER XXVIII

THE END OF THE GREAT EXPEDITION

You will remember that Captain Lewis had been accidentally wounded. He now lay helpless in the bottom of a boat; but travel by water was not especially trying, and the voyagers proceeded without any delay. They reached the country of the Mandans in due time, and there the party began to break up. One man obtained permission to return up the Missouri with some strolling traders.' The French interpreter and his wife, Sacajawea, asked to be taken no farther, and their request was granted. Their wages were paid, and they departed to their Indian friends. Sacajawea, who had so patiently borne the fatigues of the long journey, had been a wonder to the explorers. With her baby, born during the journey, and now only nineteen months old, she had traversed the whole distance without a murmur.

By dint of much persuasion, a chief, Big White by name, consented to go to Washington with the captains. He left behind him a wailing family

and many weeping friends. After cordial greetings and good-byes to their Mandan friends, a
farewell gun was fired, and the boats dropped
down to Fort Mandan. Here they found that all
the buildings but one had been accidentally burned
to the ground.

High winds and waves made their future progress dangerous, and the great changes in the bed
of the river threatened constantly to mislead them.
Where there had been sand bars two years before,
the deep current was now running. Where the
current had been deepest, islands were seen covered with willows several feet high. The traders
whom they met brought alarming reports of war
parties of Sioux, seven hundred strong. These
reports put them on their guard, but did not
retard their progress.

Early in September they met an American on
his way up the river to trade with the Indians.
He had just come from St. Louis. Nearly all
night the captains sat up and eagerly talked with
him. Think what it meant to these men to see
some one who could tell them what had been
going on in the world during the two years they
had been in the wilderness.

Three weeks later they saw some cows grazing

in a field by the river. The sight caused every man to shout for joy, for it was a sure sign that they were approaching civilization. The next day but one they touched at the gay French village of St. Charles, and were once more greeted by old acquaintances. On the 23d of September their boats glided into the Mississippi, and they soon afterward landed at St. Louis. So ended this great expedition.

Five months later Captains Lewis and Clark presented themselves in Washington with their trophies and their wonderful stock of information about the great West. The whole nation had been deeply interested in the expedition and its probable results.

Congress at once rewarded the young men with large grants of land. Within a month Captain Lewis was made governor of the great Territory of Louisiana, and a few days later Clark was made a general of militia and agent of Indian affairs. These were their nominal rewards, but could any gifts or honors truly recompense such courage, bravery, and devotion as theirs had been ?

Two years later, in 1809, Lewis was on his way from St. Louis to Washington carrying important papers. At a lonely cabin in Tennessee he stopped for the night. When morning dawned this brave and noble man lay dead. No one knows whether, worn out, anxious, and mentally depressed, he took his own life, or whether he died by another's hand. We only know that the country lost a true patriot, and a man of rare worth and ability. In the exact center of Lewis County, Tennessee, he was buried, and a broken granite shaft marks the spot. Upon this monument are cut the words written of him by Jefferson:

"*His courage was undaunted; his firmness and perseverance yielded to nothing but impossibilities. A rigid disciplinarian, yet tender as a father of those committed to his charge; honest, disinterested, liberal, with a sound understanding, and a scrupulous fidelity to truth.*"

As for William Clark, many years of usefulness followed his safe return. He seems to have been peculiarly loved by the Indians. They affectionately called him "Red Head," and St. Louis, where he made his home, was known as "Red Head's town." For seventeen years he served his country in many different capacities; but this service always brought him into close relations with the Indians. His dealings with them were marked because of their strict honor. A man of his word, he believed that word should be as sacred with the Indian as with the white man. As a consequence, with them his word was law, and his signature was, in their figurative language, "powerful medicine." He died at the age of sixty-nine. While "great as a soldier, a statesman, a diplomat, and a patriot," he was perhaps greatest as an explorer.

Of him the Indians once said in council: "We have opened our ears to your words, and those of the Red Head's brother. We receive you as the son of the Red Head. Inasmuch as we love him, we love you, and do not wish to offend you."

THE STORY OF
JOHN CHARLES FRÉMONT

JOHN CHARLES FRÉMONT

JOHN CHARLES FRÉMONT

CHAPTER I

A START IN LIFE

The father of John Charles Frémont, when a young man, was driven from his home in France by political troubles. He sailed away from his native country, hoping to find refuge in the island of San Domingo, or Haiti.

On the way across the ocean the vessel was captured by a British cruiser, and Mr. Frémont was made a prisoner of war. After some time, however, he escaped, and finally landed in America and went to the little town of Norfolk, Virginia.

There he made his living by teaching French and weaving baskets. Sometimes he earned money by decorating the ceilings of houses in an artistic fashion.

All this time he was hoping and planning to return to France.

One day he met a beautiful Virginian girl, whom

he soon married. After their marriage Mr. and Mrs. Frémont decided to travel among the Indians in the South. There were many Indians in that part of the country in 1812. There were no railroads then, and the only way of traveling was in carriages. Since there were no hotels, travelers had to carry their own beds, dishes, tents, and servants with them, and camp out.

In 1813, while Mr. and Mrs. Frémont were on one of these interesting journeys, their first son, John Charles Frémont, was born, in Savannah, Georgia.

The child's first nurses were Indian squaws, and his mother says it frightened her very much to see them hand the tiny baby about from one Indian to another. Perhaps this is one reason why John Charles Frémont was always interested in Indians, and never felt so much at home as when he was traveling.

While John Charles was still a young boy his father died, and Mrs. Frémont was left alone with her family of little children.

Mr. Frémont's brother tried to induce Mrs. Frémont to return to France with the children, as had been planned before their father's death; but Mrs. Frémont wished to remain in America among her own friends. She therefore soon removed to Charleston, South Carolina, and there made her home.

The young John Charles grew to be a large, and the writers say, a good, boy. He was unlike some other boys who became great men, notwithstanding their idleness in school; for he studied with all his might, and learned more quickly than any other boy in his class.

He mastered the most important rules of Latin in three weeks, and did equally good work in Greek and mathematics.

It was very easy for him to commit to memory chapter after chapter from the Bible. He sometimes learned three hundred verses by heart in a day.

There were two books which he always dearly loved: one was called " The Lives of Great and Daring Men," and the other was a Dutch book on astronomy. He could not read one word of the Dutch, but he pored over the maps and mathematical calculations, and in some way managed to learn a great deal about the stars.

Many great and famous people came to his mother's home, and their interesting lives made him wish to do great things himself. Of course his mother had many plans for his future.

She hoped he would become a minister; but about this time he made one or two friends, with whom he went sailing and picnicking so often that his studies were neglected, and he was finally suspended from school.

I do not know whether the young man regretted this very much, but not long afterward a very dear sister died and a brother left home, and he suddenly realized that his mother needed his help and comfort. He renewed his studies at once, and worked so hard that in a short time he was made teacher of mathematics on the sloop Natchez, where David G. Farragut was then a young lieutenant. He sailed on the sloop to South America and was gone two years.

On his return John Charles Frémont was twenty years old, and had made such a fine record that the college which had expelled him gave him "honors," and allowed him to write the initials B. A. and M. A. after his name. A little later he was appointed to the frigate Independence, but declined the appointment, because he had found a more interesting kind of work.

This work was surveying the lines of two railroads to be built—one from Charleston to Savannah, the other from Charleston to Cincinnati.

Mr. Frémont had now his first taste of exploring, and he liked it very much. He tells of the good honey and milk he had to eat, and the comfortable homes of the farmers where the surveyors slept after their long days of tramping and working.

One day he was asked by the government to make a journey among the Cherokee Indians in Georgia. These Indians lived in homes of their own, which the government had given them more than fifty years before.

But now their land was becoming very valuable, and the government decided to take it away from them and remove them to some place west of the Mississippi River. Mr. Frémont was instructed to look the land over and see where it would be best to place an army, should one be needed to drive out the Indians.

CHAPTER II

FIRST WORK FOR THE GOVERNMENT

Mr. Frémont and two other men were sent out on this expedition. At the end of the first day they came to an Indian village where a great feast was being held.   The Indian men were very drunk and very ugly.

As soon as the Indian women saw the white men come into the village they hastened to conceal them in a corn-crib until their husbands should become sober.   There they spent a very wretched night, for the drunken red men made a great deal of noise, and the corn-crib was alive with rats that ran all over the travelers as soon as they lay down to sleep.

In the morning they took a bath in the river. The water was so cold that their hair froze stiff while they were bathing.   They often slept in Indian homes, or in tents beside a great camp fire. The little pigs that ran everywhere, growing fat on the chestnuts, made fine suppers for them.

Mr. Frémont liked the Cherokee Indians very much, and was sorry to see them driven from their homes.

After a few weeks his work was done and he returned home, where he learned that the government had still other duties for him to perform. President Van Buren desired him to go out to the country beween the Mississippi and Missouri rivers and obtain all the information he could about its resources and its people.   He was to go with a Mr.

Nicollet, who was a fine scholar and an experienced explorer.

Mr. Nicollet and Mr. Frémont met in St. Louis, where they were to obtain supplies and men for the journey.

This city at that time was the starting-place for every one who was going West, and a quaint and interesting place it must have been.

The houses stood far back from the street, in great shady yards, and were built with two porches, one above the other, called galleries.

On these galleries the people spent much of their time. Here they would have their early breakfasts of coffee, bread, and fruit, and here chairs were always set for friends and visitors.

There were no pavements in the streets, and throngs of Indians, Mexicans, trappers, hunters, priests, soldiers, and gay French people moved and loitered among the locust trees that lined the streets.

Here our friends stayed a short time, collecting the things needed for their journey. At last, when everything was ready, they left St. Louis for Fort Snelling, which was then on the border of the Indian lands in Minnesota.

At Fort Snelling they spent much time in putting their instruments in order. They carried chronometers, thermometers, barometers, and tele-scopes with them, and also some instruments they could not understand at all. They "rated" the chronometer; that is, they found out how much time it lost or gained in a day. They also tested the other instruments, to make sure they were correct.

Then they set off by land with all their supplies in one-horse carts. They drove slowly along the banks of the Minnesota River, drawing maps, sketching the curious things they saw, and outlining the river's course.

Each man had his work.

One asked about the lakes and rivers, and learned their Indian names. Another collected specimens of plants. Mr. Frémont sometimes prospected for minerals and watched the stars, and made astronomical observations.

Day after day they traveled on. Indians fol-lowed them, and they found it necessary to be on their guard day and night, lest some of them might be unfriendly.

They visited the red pipe-stone quarry. This red stone was very precious to the Indians. They made their pipes and images of it, and all tribes were permitted to use it, even when they were at war with the Sioux, in whose land it lay. The Indians said that the "Spirit of the Quarry" always spoke in thunder and lightning to those who visited the quarry; and when our party arrived there they were drenched by a heavy thunder-shower, which burst upon them as if the Spirit were indeed angry.

Now they turned north. The Indians received them kindly wherever they went, and often tried to entertain them with games and hunts.

In one great hunt all the inhabitants of an Indian village took part. It was arranged by a white man who was a fur-trader, and it lasted several days. Each morning all the Indians and white men rode out for the hunt, leaving the Indian women to move the camp several miles across the country to a spot chosen by the chief.

At night when the tired and hungry hunters came into the new camp they would find great fires burning. Over each fire large pieces of venison were cooking on pointed sticks, or in huge kettles filled with corn and rice.

One night the men, being aroused from their sleep, saw a prairie fire raging and rapidly approaching. They snatched brands from their camp fires, set fire to the grass nearest to them, and quickly cleared a large space around their tents.

Over this clear space the rushing flames leaped, and when the campers dared to look up they saw that the fire had passed on, and was roaring and crackling in a grove of trees not far away.

Soon after this the party returned to St. Louis to get ready for another expedition that was to be undertaken the following year. On this new expedition they intended to explore the Missouri Valley and the great Northwest.

CHAPTER III

SECOND EXPEDITION WITH NICOLLET

Early in April, 1839, Mr. Frémont and his party left St. Louis in a small steamer. This vessel made its trips up the Missouri every year when the river was swollen by the spring rains, and on its return to St. Louis it brought the furs which the traders had collected during the winter from the Indians.

After a journey of thirteen hundred miles our explorers reached the heart of the Indian country and left the river for the land. There were nineteen men, thirty-three horses, and ten carts in the party.

On the first day of their land journey they came in sight of a great herd of buffaloes. Instantly the buffalo horses were made ready, guns were snatched up, and the hunters, dressed as lightly as possible, rode swiftly toward the lumbering beasts, keeping well out of sight and smell.

The herd was moving slowly along, feeding and grunting, as buffaloes always do when eating. As soon as they discovered the men, the buffaloes plunged headlong toward the river. But each hunter had chosen his, buffalo, and he followed him until he had killed him.

In the dust and rush, Mr. Frémont lost sight of his companions, and after killing his buffalo, sat down to rest. When he started on again he could see no sign of human beings. He was lost on the prairies.

When night came he walked in the darkness, following the tracks of the buffaloes and looking for signs of the camp. At last the gleam of a rocket far up in the sky told him that he was missed at camp, and showed him where it lay. But it was fifteen miles away! Laying his gun down so that it pointed toward the place where the rocket had been seen, Mr. Frémont brought water in his hat to his horse, unsaddled him, and using the saddle for his own pillow, lay down and slept soundly till morning.

He started early for the camp. As he rode rapidly along he saw three men on horseback galloping furiously toward him. They did not draw rein when they saw him, but rode faster than ever. The one who was ahead rode straight at Mr. Frémont, touched his sleeve, and then suddenly brought his horse to a full stop. By this he earned the large reward which Mr. Nicollet had promised to the man who should first touch the lost hunter.

This was Mr. Frémont's first buffalo hunt. The country was covered with herds of buffaloes, and their manner of living was full of interest.

The men noticed that when it was cold and snowy the herds kept moving. This was because the buffaloes on the edge of the herd were trying to get into the middle, where they would be kept warmer by the heat from one another's bodies. The buffaloes in the middle would fight to stay where they were, and so the whole herd was kept from freezing by the continual struggle.

For days our party moved along with the great beasts always in sight.

They rode through the herd by day and were encircled by it at night. The Indians organized grand hunts, to which the white men were often invited, and in turn the Indians were one day invited to dine with the explorers.

At this queer dinner party, each guest was seated on a buffalo skin and given a tin plate and spoon.

The Indians sat very still until all the tin plates were filled with a stew of buffalo meat and rice. Each chief silently tasted the stew, then solemnly laid down his spoon and looked at his next neighbor in a very strange way.

They thought the stew had been poisoned, for the cook had flavored it with some cheese, and that was a kind of food which they had never tasted. But when the cheese was shown them, and they were told that the white men could eat it unharmed, they ate it even if they did not like it.

For dessert, water sweetened with molasses was served in large iron kettles, and this the Indians liked very much.

Leaving these good friends, our men put some

green veils around the brims of their straw hats to keep away mosquitoes, packed their goods, and rode away toward Devil's Lake.

This lake was called the "Heart of the Enchanted Water" by the Indians, and there our party remained a few days, drawing some maps and writing a description of the country. By looking in your geography you will find that Devil's Lake is in the northern part of the present state of North Dakota.

This was to be the northern limit of their journey, and after exploring the shores of the lake they turned east, making their way by the easiest route to the Red River of the North. Up this river they traveled, carefully examining the country and making many sketches.

The prairies were covered with flowers, white settlers were frequently seen, and in November they arrived at Prairie du Chien, on the Mississippi River. Here they found a little steamboat ready to carry them to St. Louis, but the men were tired and decided to rest a day and take the next boat down the river.

In the morning the river was frozen from bank to bank, and the next boat would not come until the following spring. To reach home they must now travel on foot. That one day's wait caused them weeks of weary plodding over the snow-covered prairies of Illinois before they finally arrived at St. Louis.

CHAPTER IV

MARRIAGE

The President was very much pleased with the reports which Nicollet and Frémont brought back of the rich country, beautiful lakes, and navigable rivers they had explored.

There were many discussions in Congress as to whether it would be worth while to try to settle this land with white people.

Bills were introduced urging the founding of a colony at the mouth of the Columbia River, in order to protect American interests in the fur and whale trade of the Pacific Ocean. The government also hoped to establish a route to Asia through some Western port.

In the mean while, Mr. Frémont and Mr. Nicollet were hard at work on their reports and maps. All this work was done in Washington, and many senators and other public men were so interested

in it that they often came to see Mr. Nicollet and
Mr. Frémont.

Among these men was Senator Benton of Missouri. Senator Benton was a broad-minded and
earnest man, full of great plans for his country.
He believed this vast Western country was well
worth keeping for the United States.

He thought always of the western route to
Asia, and he used to say, pointing to the west:

"There lies the East; there lies the road to
India."

Day after day he went to the rooms where the
young men were at work, pored over their maps,
examined their collections of plants, animals, and
minerals, and asked many questions. He believed
in these young men, and was planning to have
them sent out on still more important expeditions.

Senator Benton often invited Mr. Frémont to
his home. Here the young man met Miss Jessie
Benton, who was a charming young girl, not yet
out of school. Mr. Frémont wished to marry her,
but she was very young, and her family, although
they admired the young man, would not consent
because of her youth.

Just at this time Mr. Frémont was suddenly
sent away to explore the Des Moines River. This

he did with great dispatch and success, and upon his return to Washington he was married to Miss Benton at the home of a mutual friend.

This marriage proved to be a very happy one. Mrs. Frémont sympathized with her husband in all his plans and work. She wrote for him, suggested new ideas, and with perfect success conducted his business when

JESSIE BENTON FRÉMONT, 1901

he was away. She showed herself to be not only a young woman of great beauty and charm, but a very intelligent one as well.

In his journal Mr. Frémont says: "Her qualities were all womanly, and education had curiously preserved the dower of a modesty which was innate. There had been no experience of life to brush away the bloom. There was a rare union of intelligence to feel the injury of events, and submission to bear them in silence and discretion; and withal a sweet and happy and forbearing temper which has remained proof against the wearing of time."

CHAPTER V

FIRST INDEPENDENT WESTERN EXPEDITION

The government finally decided to send out an exploring party to the Far West as "an aid to the emigration to the Lower Columbia."

It was expected that Mr. Nicollet would be the leader, but he was too ill to accept the appointment, and the command was therefore given to Mr. Frémont.

He was to examine the line of western travel, and carefully describe it. He was also to select positions for forts. He was to go as far west as the South Pass, discovered by Lewis and Clark, and used by all travelers to the Columbia River.

This pass was near the source of the Platte River, in the western part of what is now the state of Wyoming. The journey was to end there, and the expedition was to return to Washington.

The news of his appointment to this responsible position reached Mr. Frémont on New-Year's Day, 1842. The following May, seven months after his marriage, and when Mr. Frémont was only twenty-nine years old, he started on this journey.

KIT CARSON

From St. Louis he went by steamboat to the mouth of the Kansas River.

On the boat he met the famous scout, Kit Carson, who had just been to St. Louis to place his little daughter in school. The two became good friends, and Mr. Frémont persuaded Kit Carson to act as the guide on the expedition.

They landed at "Chouteaus," near the mouth of the Kansas River, and spent twenty days making preparations for the overland journey. On the 10th of June, 1842, everything was ready. The party was armed and mounted. Eight men drove the eight baggage-carts, filled with provisions, gifts, and instruments. Each cart was drawn by two mules. A few extra horses and oxen straggled along behind, to be used in case of necessity.

At first they passed many Indian farms, but were soon on the open prairie, which stretched before them like an ocean.

When night came on the party halted. The eight carts were placed in the form of a circle, the tents were pitched, and the horses were turned out to grass. The four cooks built their fires and prepared the supper.

As it grew dark the horses were tied by long ropes to stakes driven into the ground, a guard was mounted, and the tired men fell asleep.

At the first streak of daylight the men were up, the horses were fed, breakfast was eaten, and by seven o'clock all were in line, moving west. Rainy days, hot days, cool days, sunny days, followed each other rapidly, and the journey went regularly on.

Among their supplies was a rubber boat; this they used to carry their wagons across the rivers. One day, after six of the wagons had been safely ferried across a small river, Mr. Frémont decided to put the other two into the boat at one time, for it was nearly night. The wagons were safely loaded, a man took the line in his teeth and swam ahead to help pull the boat across, when suddenly the load capsized, and boxes and barrels went gayly floating down stream.

The men leaped into the water, and managed to save everything but a bag of coffee and a large quantity of sugar, which of course dissolved.

The Indians were friendly, and brought coffee, vegetables, and butter to the party; for they were used to the emigrant trains which often traveled along this route.

One day, however, our men were alarmed by a shout of "Indians!" Kit Carson leaped to his feet, sprang bareheaded upon his unsaddled horse, and galloped away to investigate. In a few minutes he came back to tell the men that the Indians were only elks quietly feeding.

On the morning of July 4th the explorers were

entertained by a race, which was more exciting than Fourth of July races usually are.

The men were at breakfast, when suddenly a buffalo calf landed in the midst of the camp, hotly chased by two wolves. The wolves ran around the camp; the calf went through it. This gave him a little better chance, for he was making a straight dash for a herd two miles distant. But soon another wolf joined the chase, then another and another, until there were twenty or thirty of them, and the poor calf was overtaken, and half eaten before he was dead.

CHAPTER VI

THE PARTY DIVIDED

In order to explore the country more thoroughly the party was now divided, and started in different directions to meet at South Pass.

It was a hard journey for all, for the days were hot, the sand was deep, food poor, and water scarce.

At night Mr. Frémont set up his little waterproof tent around three guns tied together. This made a very small tent, but under it the instruments were put, and then Mr. Frémont himself would lie down with his head among the instruments. If it rained, his head at least was dry.

Just before they came to Fort Laramie they found that not all Indians were so friendly as those they had formerly met. A party of two or three hundred were on the point of attacking the white men, when the foremost Indian was recognized by one of Frémont's men, and the whole party of braves swept by like the wind.

The fact that there were a good many forts through this part of the country probably served to hold the Indians in check.

These forts were queerly but wisely built. First a mud wall was made about fifteen feet high. On top of this stakes were driven as close together as possible. The outside walls were really the backs of the houses, which were built around a hollow square. On two of the corners of the inclosure towers were built, and over the gateway was another tower. The houses had windows opening upon the inclosed square, and there the fur-traders lived with their wives and children.

Our party remained at Fort Laramie for several days. Wild stories of the Indians came to them.

The men were badly frightened, and even Kit Carson made his will. But Mr. Frémont felt that he must complete the exploration as it had been planned, and rallying the men about him, he urged those who were afraid to remain behind. Only one man refused to go on. The rest were ready to follow their leader anywhere.

The explorers were now beset with many difficulties. Some of their instruments were lost. They had no bread of any kind, and their only food was buffalo meat, which had been cooked, covered with tallow, and packed into bags. It looked and tasted like pieces of wood.

At length they reached the mountains and began the ascent. The sure-footed mules carried the men safely from rock to rock. Up and up they climbed till they came to the snow line.

Frémont was the first one to reach the crest, where from the top of a cliff which was almost perpendicular, he looked down into a snow-field five hundred feet below him.

The point on which he stood was only a tiny ledge. It was the summit of one of the highest mountains in the range, the mountain which is still called "Frémont's Peak." There he planted the Stars and Stripes.

From this great height he overlooked "innumerable lakes and springs. On one side was the source of the Colorado of the West, and on the other the Wind River Valley, where were the heads of the Yellowstone branch of the Missouri. Far to the north he could discover the sunny heads of the Trois Tetons, where were the sources of the Missouri and Columbia rivers. And on the southern extremity of the ridge the peaks were plainly visible, among which are found some of the headsprings of the Nebraska or Platte rivers."

The explorers descended the mountain and continued their journey homeward. Down the Sweetwater and the Platte they went, using their rubber boat whenever they could.

At some places the current was very strong and rapid as it plunged through some deep gulch or cañon. In one of these cañons they came to grief. The men had been struggling all day to hold the boat back and keep it off the rocks, but it finally broke away, cleared rock after rock, shot over one fall after another, threw the men into the water, and finally capsized entirely.

Without guns or ammunition, soaking wet, and barefooted, the explorers clambered up the rocks and went on, leaving one man to recover the boat as best he could.

At a point a little lower down they returned to the river and embarked upon it in a "bull boat."

These boats were made in a curious way. Buffalo skins were sewed together and stretched over a willow frame. The seams were calked with a mixture of ashes and tallow, and the boat was dried a day or two in the sun. All this work was useless, however, for the river was no longer navigable, and the "bull boat" was abandoned on the river's bank.

The Missouri was finally reached. Horses and carts were sold, a boat was made ready, and the explorers were soon floating rapidly toward the longed-for harbor at St. Louis. Just five months after his departure, Mr. Frémont was again in Washington.

CHAPTER VII

SECOND INDEPENDENT EXPEDITION

Almost before the reports of his former expedition were prepared, a plan was perfected for another one. This time Mr. Frémont was to proceed to South Pass by a new route; and from that place he was to explore the country south of the Columbia River between the Rocky Mountains and the Pacific Ocean.

Early in 1843, he and Mrs. Frémont left for St. Louis. The new expedition was to be equipped on a larger scale than any that had preceded it.

There were thirty-nine men in the party, and their supplies were packed into twelve mule-carts, while a light wagon carried the instruments. A small howitzer was a new feature of the outfit, and a mill for grinding grain was also taken along.

The objects which were to be attained by this expedition were, first, to find some new route to Oregon and California, and second, to explore thoroughly the Arkansas River to its sources.

During the first part of the journey they knew just what was before them. There were streams to be bridged or forded; there was game to be killed; there were Indians to be watched, plants to be gathered, sketches to be drawn, and observations to be taken.

As they approached the Rocky Mountains the country became dry and sandy; the rivers grew shallow and dropped out of sight in the sand; and the mountains lifted themselves in the distance, "grand and luminously white, covered to their bases with glittering snow."

They passed within full view of Pike's Peak, and food being scarce, they turned a little to the right in the hope of finding better supplies. One morning they surprised a grizzly bear that was hard at work digging up a breakfast of roots.

When the animal saw the men he charged upon them so suddenly that their horses in shying almost pitched them from their saddles. One shot struck the bear—again he charged. Another shot —another charge, until the sixth shot put an end to the fight.

After many weary days of travel the explorers at length arrived at Great Salt Lake. This lake had never been visited except by Indians or trappers. Not far from its shores the explorers discovered some hot springs which threw their steaming waters many feet into the air. The ground gave out a rumbling sound and seemed on the point of bursting open. It was a strange and interesting place, and one did not wonder that the Indians believed the land bewitched.

The Great Salt Lake did not prove to be so dreadful as they had anticipated. The rubber boat was unpacked and prepared for service, and

PIKE'S PEAK

the men discussed their proposed voyage on the lake as they sat about their supper of roots and a small duck some one had secured.

The next morning the rubber boat was launched, and the day was spent in drifting down a little creek which flowed into the lake. Thousands of birds flew about them, and the air seemed full of plovers.

But the water was so shallow they were obliged to drag the boat for a mile through ill-smelling mud. Suddenly they found that the water was so salty that it stung the tongue to taste it. And now, to their distress, the boat sprang a leak. The waves began to rise, spray flew over them, their hands and clothes were covered with salt. Finally they were forced to land on a large island.

That night they were obliged to camp in a place so low and swampy that willow branches were piled on the ground to keep them out of the mud and water. But they supped royally on roast ducks and geese, and slept soundly on the willows.

The next day they returned to the mainland safely, and at once made plans to secure a new supply of salt. They had had none for a long time, but here they could easily get all they wanted.

From Great Salt Lake our explorers proceeded

to what is now the southeast corner of the state of Washington.   They were then a thousand miles from South Pass, and two thousand miles from St. Louis.

Mount Hood was in sight, and toward that snowy height they moved along the banks of the wonderful Columbia River, with its cañons and rapids.   Emigrants had been coming into this region for several years, and all about our travelers were signs of civilization.

They passed within hearing of the great falls of the Columbia, which Lewis and Clark had been the first to discover, and there they saw the same tribes of dirty and degraded savages.

One fine day they came upon a schoolhouse and a mission station.   There a number of canoes were procured, and the tired explorers embarked upon the stream.   Down the great Columbia they sped, arriving in due time at Fort Vancouver, the western limit of their long journey.

It would have been a great pleasure to Mr. Frémont to see the Pacific, but he was under orders and felt he had no right to go farther.   So after a short delay the homeward journey was begun.

CHAPTER VIII

IN THE FAR NORTHWEST

Mr. Frémont was a very strong man. It is said that he always used a wooden saddle with no covering at all, and that he could ride farther than any of his men without resting. A story is told of his riding eight hundred miles in eight days.

No matter how cold it might be, he never wore an overcoat. His men said that on some nights he would sit for hours in the snow when the thermometer showed twenty or thirty degrees below zero, waiting for a star to arrive at the exact point for an observation.

He had need of all his strength and endurance.

The weather on the Columbia was cold and wet. Heavy fog that turned to water when it touched the hair or face hung over them day and night.

The path grew more and more rugged until the mountains were crossed. Then the weather became sunny and beautiful, and the river was suddenly very interesting.

The great mountain peaks of Rainier, St. Helen's, and Mount Hood were successively in sight, as the explorers forded streams and clambered over jagged bowlders.

While crossing one of these streams the mule that was carrying the sugar fell, and the sugar became molasses at once. This was a loss which the men sincerely mourned.

At intervals they passed the curious huts of the Klamath Indians. These huts had rounded roofs, through which the family or visitor entered. Hung inside of these roofs were strings of smoked and dried fish. The people wore odd-looking shoes, made of straw and grass, baskets for caps, and shells for nose ornaments.

No guides could be secured from these Indians, and the party pressed on over the mountains, floundering through deep snow, and coaxing the animals to follow them.

Finally they arrived at the crest of the range, and standing in snow three feet deep, they looked down a thousand feet into a beautiful lake surrounded by green fields and fertile hills.

It was no easy matter to get down to this lake. The way was so steep that one of the mules lost its footing, and rolled two or three hundred feet into a ravine without being hurt at all.

At times the water was so full of salt that the

men went without food, because there was no water with which to cook it.   At other times they would dig deep holes in the ground, and filter the water; and though it was still very bad, it could then be used for cooking.   On Christmas Day they managed to make some salty coffee, in which there was a little sugar.   This was a fine feast for them.

Indians were always in sight, the country was a desert, the horses' feet were cut to pieces on the rocks, water was always scarce, and New-Year's Day found the explorers very wretched indeed.

All these hardships made Frémont decide to pass over the Sierra Nevada Mountains, and attempt to enter the Sacramento Valley.

CHAPTER IX

OVER THE SIERRA NEVADAS

The Indians skimmed about our party day after day on their snowshoes.   They were not afraid of the guns of the white men.   Hiding behind rocks, these Indians laughed at the white men floundering in the snow, while they glided along as easily as if on wings.

From these Indians Mr. Frémont learned that

they had not been crossing the mountains at all, but traveling along the crest of a range which formed the western edge of the great American Basin.

To reach the coast there was still another mountain range to cross.

The Indians said that the men could never cross the mountains so late in the season. They drew their hands across their necks and above their heads, to show that the snow would bury them. They shut their eyes and shook their heads, to say they knew nothing of the terrible way ahead, and could not guide the white men.

At last a splendid young Indian consented to lead the way. Frémont gave him some fine, gay clothes, and he made a brilliant picture as he stalked ahead. Behind him one man came leading a horse and breaking a path for those who followed. When this man became exhausted he would drop behind and the next man and horse would take his place.

The horses began to fail. Their packs were thrown away, but even then they had no strength to climb. The snow grew deeper. The trail was strewn with camp belongings. Their way led, as one old Indian had told them it would, over "rock upon rock, rock upon rock, snow upon snow, snow upon snow." The nights were so cold they could not sleep. The guide threw his gay blanket over his head and began to wail.

The end seemed near, when a small party that had gone ahead on snowshoes suddenly discovered the valley which they were seeking lying far below them.

Miles of snow stretched before them, but they now knew where they were, and hope revived. Dreadful days followed, as, faint with hunger and fatigue, and blinded by the snow, they pressed on, slowly dragging their sledges of supplies and urging on their starving animals. They little realized that eighty miles of distress and misery must still be passed before they reached their journey's end.

CHAPTER X

THE DESCENT INTO THE VALLEY

Although the men were full of hope they found the drifts as deep as ever. They used axes and mauls to pack the snow so that it would support the weight of their animals. The men themselves crawled along on their hands and knees.

In crossing a frozen stream Mr. Frémont slipped, broke through the ice, and fell into deep water. Kit Carson plunged in to pull him out, and both men splashed to the bank, where they built a fire and dried their dripping clothes.

A few days more of agony, and the valley was reached. It seemed like heaven to the men as they feasted on a supper of boiled mule meat. They were wild with delight at the sight of grass, budding branches, butterflies, and flowers.

One poor man lost his reason and wandered away into the woods. He never returned. Two other men were gone for days, but finally struggled back to camp more dead than alive.

A night's rest in an adobe house refreshed the explorers, who went back over their trail the next day to meet some of their companions who had fallen behind.

Lean, ragged, and thin, the poor fellows came in. Only thirty-three of their sixty-seven horses survived to reach the valley.

How the explorers enjoyed the lovely scene before them after their terrible journey through the mountains! Here was a comfortable house built of sun-dried brick, low and yellow. Large wheatfields stretched on all sides. Indian men were plowing and Indian girls carrying water to the gardens.

This place was the ranch of a certain Captain Sutter, and was very famous in that day. Cap-

SUTTER'S FORT

tain Sutter's residence consisted of several low adobe houses built around a hollow square.

The backs of these houses formed the wall of the fort, on top of which were twelve pieces of artillery. Within the houses were quarters for the soldiers, blacksmith and other shops, a distillery, and the dwelling of Captain Sutter.

After resting here for nearly a month, the re-

freshed explorers renewed their march, directing
their course southward. They hoped, by going
that way, to avoid the severe mountain journey
and to cross the San Joaquin Valley.

From the San Joaquin they would follow the
Los Angeles trail to Santa Fé in New Mexico,
then move northeast to the head waters of the
Arkansas River, whence they could easily return
to St. Louis.

CHAPTER XI

HOMEWARD

For days they traveled through the lovely California country. To breathe was a pleasure, and
the men looked with delight upon the fields of
gorgeous poppies, the delicate mariposa lilies, and
the blossoming trees.

The scouts moved ahead, the "pack animals,
baggage, and the horned cattle being in the center." The advance and rear guards were com-
posed of Indians, Germans, French, Spanish, and
Americans. Slowly they trailed along, through a
land that seemed a paradise on earth, until one
day a great shout announced that they had reached
the "Spanish trail."

To-day in the vestibuled trains of the Santa Fé railroad we follow this very line of the Spanish trail. In those days it was a dangerous journey, for the land was swarming with hostile Indians, there was only a narrow trail through the desert, and there was almost no water.

One day a band of hostile savages drove off the horses belonging to Mr. Frémont's party. Three men started in hot pursuit. One horse gave out, but the other two riders tore along the trail, found the horses, attacked, killed, and scalped two of the thieves, and drove away the others.

Some of the horses had been killed, and their flesh was already boiling in great kettles, preparatory to a great feast. But the party was broken up, and the refreshments (in the shape of the rest of the horses) were driven back to their owners.

The desert stretched on all sides. Deposits of alkali lay like light snow on the ground, hurting the eyes and the skin. The water, when found, was unfit to drink, and almost every step of the way was marked, as it is to-day, with the bleaching bones of poor animals that could not stand the dreadful journey.

How the sun beat down! The men chewed the leaves of the sand plants to moisten their dry

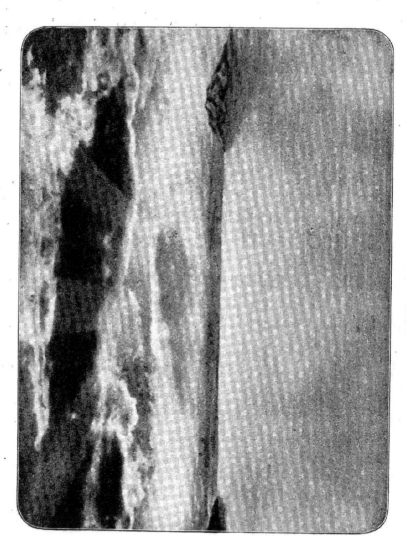

GREAT SALT LAKE

mouths, and were always on guard lest the Indians should swoop down upon them.

In May they touched the shores of Great Salt Lake, which they had left in the preceding September. In the intervening months they had traversed a circuit of three thousand five hundred miles, and made a map of the West a possible thing.

From Great Salt Lake the way was well known. Pike's Peak once more loomed in sight. Their familiar friends, the buffaloes, were about them.

At the end of a few days they reached the point where Kansas City now stands. Thence a tiny steamer carried them down the muddy Missouri to St. Louis, and another great journey was successfully completed.

CHAPTER XII

TROUBLE WITH THE MEXICANS

The reports which Mr. Frémont brought back of the lovely climate of California, the beautiful scenery, the fertile lands, the huge trees, the broad grassy plains, and the fields of grain, made many people wish to go there.

The government felt that California must be acquired from Mexico, if possible, in "an honorable and just manner." If Mexico would not give it up willingly, it must be acquired by force. Reports began to be heard that Mexico was preparing for war.

Just at this time Mr. Frémont was again sent out. He was to travel over much of the same ground as on other journeys, and he was to watch closely the interests of the United States.

The party was to go to the head waters of the Arkansas, Rio Grande, and Colorado rivers, touch again at Salt Lake, and cross the Cascade and Sierra Nevada ranges to find an easy pass through the mountains. Much of this was an old story to the men, and they fell into the hard work very readily.

But winter was near. The party was divided into two companies, in order to examine all the points of interest closely. One company was to go direct to Lake Tulare, the other to the same place by way of Sutter's camp.

Sutter's camp was reached by Frémont's party; but when they proceeded to Lake Tulare they found that the other division had not arrived. The Indians watched every chance to steal their horses.   The camp was closely guarded day and night.

Feeling pretty sure that all would be well, Mr. Frémont left his party, and with seven men made a call upon the Mexican authorities in Monterey. He wished to get leave to have his party refitted on Mexican soil.

. Permission was given, and for a month they rested, while everything was put in order for a longer trip.

One afternoon a Mexican cavalry officer rode into the camp. He gave some letters to Captain Frémont, signed by the Mexican official, General Castro, commanding Captain Frémont to leave the country at once.   Threats were added if he should not obey.

Captain Frémont replied that both he and his country had been insulted, and he would not leave.   He moved his camp to a hill near by, where there was plenty of grass and water, and a fine view of the country on all sides.   He built a rough fort of logs, and hoisted the American flag above it.   The party remained there for three days, while a force of Mexican soldiers was gathering in the valley below.

On the third day the flag accidentally fell; but

as no attack had been made, Captain Frémont decided to move on. But the order from the Mexican government seemed very strange.

The American consul sent letters to Washington, asking for instructions. He asked the commanders of American war vessels at San Blas, or Mazatlan, to send a ship to Monterey at once.

Everything seemed quiet, however, and Captain Frémont moved on up the Sacramento Valley. Mount Shasta soon came in sight. The fields were covered with poppies. Frightened bands of antelopes hurtled through the bushes, and deer fled when they saw the men coming.

The weather was perfect, and there seemed nothing unpleasant at hand. But these easy days were only the calm before the breaking of the storm.

CHAPTER XIII

A GOVERNMENT MESSAGE

As Captain Frémont was standing alone by his camp fire one night, thinking of his work and enjoying the warm blaze under the chilly shadow of the mountain, he heard the sound of horses' feet. His own horses were quietly grazing. Indians would never come in such a fashion. What could it mean?

As he stood listening intently, two men on horseback rode wearily into the circle of firelight. Frémont had known them both. They had ridden hard, a hundred miles, to inform him of the coming of a messenger with letters from Washington. They feared this messenger had been killed, for the Indians were known to be skulking near.

Nothing could be done that night, but at dawn a strong and fearless party of men were sent to find the messenger, Captain Gillespie.

They met him at nightfall. Our men had not heard from home for eleven months, and they knew this messenger must have important news to have followed them so far.

Captain Gillespie told them that the United States was on the point of going to war with Mexico, and that Frémont, the explorer, was now to do all he could to secure California for the United States.

He was to learn what the men of California wanted, and whether they were friendly toward the

United States. He was to learn what he could of England's plans regarding California; and he was to act as he thought best for the good of the United States.

Late at night Frémont sat alone by the low-burning camp fire, excited by the news, and considering what should be done.

He re-read the letters and tried to interpret their meaning. At last he made up his mind that the government meant to say to him: "The time has come. England must not get a foothold in California. We must be first; act discreetly, but positively."

The messenger, Gillespie, was directed to act in concert with Frémont.

The plan was to secure California before any foreign vessel could arrive in her ports.

Just as this was coming clearly into his mind, there was a sudden and frightened movement among the horses and mules. Taking his revolver in his hand, Captain Frémont went out among them. The mules had stopped eating, and stood listening, with their long ears stuck straight out in front of them.

Now, mules are good sentinels, and their conduct betokened the presence of Indians; but none

could be found, and Captain Frémont went back
to the fire and his letters.

Once more he considered every possible plan.
Remembering his instructions when he left Washington, and knowing that the United States government wished to make the Pacific Ocean its
western boundary, he decided to go back to the
Sacramento Valley. As he was the only army
officer in California, he would make his party a
small army of conquest.

Having thus made up his mind, Captain Frémont wrapped his blankets about him, and crept
under the low-spreading branches of a cedar tree
to sleep.

Just as he fell into a doze a shout from Kit
Carson aroused him. The camp was astir with
excitement. Startled from their sleep by a dull
thud, the explorers had found two of their party
dead, with tomahawks buried in their heads.

White men and Indians snatched their rifles
just as a band of savages made an attack upon the
camp. The fires were smoldering.

"We hung blankets to the cedar boughs and
bushes near by, for a defense against the arrows,"
says Captain Frémont. "The Indians continued
to pour in their arrows. Every movement on

their part brought a rifle shot from us. All night we lay behind our blanket defenses, with our rifles cocked in our hands, expecting another attack, until the morning light enabled us to see that the Indians had disappeared. By their tracks we found that fifteen or twenty Klamaths had attacked us."

This attack was very hard to forgive, because Captain Frémont had given these very Indians friendly presents, and divided the only food he had with them but a few days before.

Among Frémont's men were some Indians who were deadly enemies of these Klamath Indians, and they were determined to have revenge. The party cleaned their rifles, and started in grim pursuit. The whole country was astir, and Indians on all sides were gathering for battle.

The men continued to pursue the Indians for days, and their rifles had need to be quick and ready to ward off the poisoned arrows of the savages.

As Captain Frémont and Kit Carson were riding along together one day they came full upon an Indian, his arrow drawn to the head and aimed at Carson. Captain Fremont fired instantly, but missed, and Kit Carson would have been a dead man had it not been for Frémont's horse Sacramento.

This horse was a wonderful creature. He had carried his master thousands of miles, and seemed to have as much intelligence as a man. Sacramento sprang full at the Indian, knocked him down, and the man who rode behind dispatched the savage at once.

CHAPTER XIV

FRÉMONT'S WAR

Captain Frémont believed that the Indians wished the English to get California from the Mexicans. He felt that these Indians were hostile to the United States, for his own party was constantly being attacked by them. He also learned that the English were furnishing the Indians with arrowheads and tomahawks.

So he wrote a letter to Senator Benton, telling him that he thought the English should be driven at once from the posts they held, otherwise they might be expected to become masters in California.

He then wrote to the commander of an American war vessel in the harbor of Monterey, asking for supplies for his party. These supplies were received, together with a letter offering Captain Frémont any help he might need.

News came soon afterward that the Indians were gathering in the mountains, prepared for war. It was also said that the Indians were being urged to burn the crops of the American settlers.

The settlers begged Captain Frémont to protect them, and they also sent a petition to the American war vessels lying at anchor in the harbors.

Protection was promised the settlers, when a message came from some Mexicans, saying they were willing to organize a separate government in California, under a foreign power, but they were not willing that the United States should be that power. All this was in the fall of 1845.

In view of these rumors and the fears of the American settlers, Captain Frémont moved his camp among the buttes of the Sacramento, and there the Americans gathered to tell of their troubles and to protect themselves in case of any outbreak.

The grain fields were ready for the harvest. The firing of them was expected any moment.

The Mexican General Castro was collecting droves of horses. One of these droves was captured by Frémont's men. War seemed unavoidable, and Captain Frémont decided to strike the first blow.

He has been severely criticized for this. Many people felt that he should have waited for explicit orders from Washington, but no one in Washington could possibly know the condition of affairs as Captain Frémont knew them. At all events, his decision was made.

Riding rapidly out of camp along the banks of the Sacramento, he surprised the Indians, who were dressed in war-paint and feathers, and were performing their war ceremonies.

The Indians ran for their lives, jumped into the river, and swam for shelter. One Indian camp after another was visited, and the river was soon thickly dotted with the heads of the escaping Indians.

These Indians had their own farms and homes. Their enemies lived both in the mountains and the plains. The safest place for them was in their own homes. Captain Frémont believed they would soon return to these homes, and give no more trouble. He accordingly withdrew his men to Santa Barbara.

There the ship Portsmouth, commanded by Captain Montgomery, was to meet him. About this time one of Captain Frémont's men, whom he called his field-marshal, came to camp with a number of Mexican prisoners, captured at Sonoma by a party of California settlers.

Captain Frémont realized fully that he was in a strange position. One of the men in his command had made prisoners of Mexicans. This would be to Mexico a just cause for war with the United States. He could show no written orders from his government for such an act, but he was proceeding as if he had these orders. The naval officers were also assisting him.

He believed that but one honorable course lay open for him, and that was to resign his position as an officer in the army of the United States. He did this at once.

Another event occurred at this period which also had a marked influence upon his course of action. A man named Ide had issued a proclamation, declaring California an independent republic. As the new republic must have a flag, he made one of a piece of white cloth, on which the figure of a grizzly bear was painted with berry juice.

This gave the name of the " Bear Flag War " to these fights of Frémont with the Mexicans.

It was rumored also that all Americans had been ordered to leave Sacramento, taking nothing with them. Two Americans were murdered.

This was more than Frémont could endure. He could not understand why the United States government did not send orders for the conduct of its officers in California.

He at once organized an armed party, proceeded to the south side of San Francisco Bay, captured a fort there, spiked the Spanish guns, and quickly returned to camp. Mexican authority was now at an end in the territory north of San Francisco Bay, and as far inland as Sutter's Fort.

Uniting with him some four hundred men who promptly elected him their leader, Frémont was prepared to defend the ground already taken.

Word was received from Captain Montgomery that an American flag was flying at Monterey, and that another had been sent to Sonoma. He asked Frémont to raise one at Sutter's Fort. This was done with a salute of twenty-one guns, and amid the rejoicing of the people.

The Bear Flag War was over, the Mexican

government had lost California, and the United States had gained it.

At length Frémont received orders from Stockton to proceed to Monterey. This he did. At Monterey he embarked with his men for San Diego, where he hoped to head off General Castro of Mexico, and overthrow his authority in Los Angeles.

Frémont now held the office of major by Stockton's appointment, and acted under his orders.

The Mexican officers at San Diego received Major Frémont and his men kindly; and the band started north toward Los Angeles. They were charmed with the wonderful climate. Great orchards of peaches, olives, and pears covered the land, as they do to-day.

At Los Angeles they were met by Stockton, and entered the city in fine style. General Castro could not be found. He had buried his guns, dispersed his men, and fled for safety.

Scouts were sent out to scour the country, and bring in any Mexican officers whom they might find. Stockton at once organized a government in the name of the United States, and appointed Frémont "military governor of the territory." He also made the messenger, Gillespie, "command-ant of the southern district."

He then told Major Frémont that he would meet him in San Francisco in October, and make him governor of California.

The work Major Frémont had done was highly praised by the President, in his annual message, as well as by the secretaries of the war and navy departments; but Congress did not recognize his work in the same manner.

Major Frémont now undertook a return march to the Sacramento Valley. Not long after his departure word came that the people in Los Angeles were in rebellion, and Major Frémont was ordered back to reduce them to subjection.

A day later, at the head of a band of 170 armed men, Major Frémont embarked on the ship Sterling, and sailed for Santa Barbara. From that place he was carried on another vessel to San Pedro, the port of Los Angeles. This vessel was delayed by heavy fogs, but as soon as Major Frémont was able to land he made great efforts to collect horses and supplies, and to enlist a larger number of men under his command.

Several battles, or skirmishes, followed; in

which Major Frémont was successful. But the struggle was nearly at an end.

Through the influence of Bernard Ruiz, a very influential and wise woman, the "capitulation of Conenga" was brought about, and by it the war was ended in California.

Orders now came for Frémont to return to Washington. He was placed under arrest, charged with mutiny, disobedience, and disorder, and commanded to report at once for trial.

At the close of that trial he was pronounced guilty, and sentenced to be dismissed from the service. The President, however, revoked the sentence, and after reproving him, retained him in the army.

The President's pardon was refused by Frémont, for he said that if he accepted pardon it would look as if he were guilty of the charges made. This he would not admit.

In May, however, he resigned his commission in the army of his own accord. This political misunderstanding did not overcome Frémont's desire for travel and exploration, and in October, 1848, he again started for the West.

CHAPTER XV

THE FOURTH EXPEDITION

Mr. Frémont was now thirty-four years old. Inspired by Senator Benton's idea that a railroad could and should be built across the Rocky Mountains, he undertook to find the best route for such an enterprise. In this expedition he had no help from the government.

Up the Arkansas River his company went, just as on a previous expedition. They saw the herds of buffaloes, elks, and antelope, passed the same tribes of Indians, and lived the same kind of life. But at the foot of the Rocky Mountains their troubles began.

Mr. Frémont had for a guide a strange man called "Bill Williams." This man had come West as a missionary to the Osage Indians. He had soon found this work not much to his liking, and had built a little hut for himself, where he lived alone, hunting and trapping in the mountains.

He was friendly with some Indians and a dreadful enemy to others. He could ride any beast, and must have made a queer figure on horseback, "leaning forward upon the pommel with his rifle before him, his stirrup ridiculously short, and his breeches rubbed up to his knees, leaving his legs bare, even in freezing weather."

He wore a loose monkey-jacket, or a buckskin hunting-shirt, and for his head-covering a blanket cap, the two top corners drawn up into two wolfish, satyr-like ears.

He loved this life, and spent all the money he made in drunken sprees. He was said to have come into Taos one day with $6,000, the earnings of a season's trapping. He spent it all, and left town a few days later deep in debt.

This was the guide whom Mr. Frémont had engaged to conduct him over the mountains.

The party entered the mountains on the 26th of November, 1848. Terrible days followed. It was so cold that the men's faces and lips were badly frozen, while their whiskers and hair stood out stiff with frost.

Snow-covered heights loomed above them; mountain streams full of ice roared across their path; the drifted snow grew deeper and deeper. Many of the mules were frozen, and dropped dead beside the trail.

The men suffered tortures. At the end of

three weeks it seemed as though they could not endure their sufferings any longer. Working with pickaxes, they could only advance half a mile a day through the snow and ice.

When fires were built the heat melted deep holes in the snow. Into these holes the men would huddle for the night, finding themselves covered with snow in the morning.

They finally decided to turn back. They were now living on the frozen bodies of the dead mules. When these were gone they made food of the raw-hide ropes and leather saddle trappings, cutting them up and cooking them to a kind of glue.

Slowly retreating, they at length reached the place on the homeward trail where they had hoped to find game. But the game had been driven away by the intense cold.

A small party had been sent ahead for relief. This party did not return, and Frémont, with a few trusted men, pushed forward to find them, ordering the others to follow as they could.

Sadly the men who were left behind struggled on, being obliged sometimes to creep forward on their hands and knees. One man prevailed upon the others to wait, perfectly still, for three days. As they lay almost dead in the snow, near the end of the third day, a great shout was heard, and a horseman rode into camp with bread in his hands.

The poor fellows cried like babies, and would have torn the man from his horse if they had had the strength. But they could not lift their hands.

Others of the rescuing party soon came up. They built a fire and cooked some corn meal, which they carefully fed to the famished men. Then they lifted them upon the horses, and returned upon their trail to their companions, who were waiting below. Twenty-three men were left of the thirty-three who had entered the mountains.

In February they reached the pueblo of Colorado, where the first small party had already arrived. Frémont hastened forward to Taos to arrange for another attempt to cross the mountains farther south. Four days later the rest of the men started for Santa Fé, leaving Williams, the guide, behind. The next spring he went into the mountains to secure the luggage left behind by Frémont's party and was killed by the Indians.

At Taos, Frémont learned of the finding of gold in California. His companions had seen traces of it several times in their journeys, but had given the matter no attention.

Frémont had long before this purchased land in Mariposa County for a home. There he built a rude house, which Mrs. Frémont afterward transformed into a delightful home, and there he began to plan what more he could do for the state he loved.

He was appointed the first senator from California, and presented a large number of bills during the short time he was in Congress.

Gold had been discovered on his own land in Mariposa County, and he and Mrs. Frémont now made a trip abroad, hoping to interest people in England and France in the development of California. He was honored by the queen of England, given a medal by the king of Prussia, and a Founder's Medal by the Royal Geographical Society of Berlin.

CHAPTER XVI

THE LAST YEARS OF LIFE

It might be expected that Frémont would have been discouraged by the frightful experience of his last journey, but he was not.

In February, 1854, he started once more, determined to prove whether it was possible to build the railroad so dear to Senator Benton's mind.

The journey was finally accomplished, and the great Santa Fé railroad is now a witness as to the thoroughness of the work that was performed.

Returning to California by the isthmus of Panama, the intrepid explorer, who had endured so many hardships, fell ill of a fever. After his recovery he took up an active outdoor life and engaged in cattle-raising.

The government needed a drove of cattle for the Indians. Mr. Frémont promised to supply them. Finding no one that could be trusted to care for the herd on its long passage across the plains, he himself made the journey of three hundred miles, and delivered the cattle.

In spite of the trying misunderstandings between himself and the government, Frémont's fame increased. Books and pamphlets in praise of him and his work were published, and in 1856 he was chosen by the Republican party as their candidate for the presidency. He stood for "no slaves," but the country was not yet ready to support this doctrine, and he was defeated by James Buchanan.

A few years later, while again abroad, the Civil

War broke out, and Frémont was made Commander of the West. The West included Illinois, and all states and territories lying west of the Mississippi River and east of the Rocky Mountains.

His headquarters were in St. Louis, which he at once fortified. He quickly collected an army, many of the men in it being those who had traveled with him. He lost a battle at Springfield, Missouri. He suppressed all newspapers disloyal to the government, and assumed to govern Missouri.

The government thought a grave error had been made at Springfield, and Frémont was relieved of his command. The particular act which caused his relief from command was an emancipation proclamation, which he issued in August, 1861. This he believed to be a military necessity, and when asked by President Lincoln to withdraw the order he refused. Thereupon the President revoked the order, and relieved Frémont of his command.

Not long after he was made commander in the mountain district of Virginia, Tennessee, and Kentucky. In 1862 he asked to be relieved, and returned to his family in New York.

Two years later he was again mentioned for

the presidency, but believing Lincoln to be the needed man, he withdrew his name. He was governor of Arizona from 1878 to 1882.

He died in New York July 13, 1890, at the age of seventy-seven years.

Such was the career of a great explorer, soldier, scholar, legislator, and public benefactor. Men still living recall his dashing bravery, his sturdy loyalty to his own opinions, his courageous heart, his admirable life. To those who knew him, these words of the one who understood him best seem but just praise: "He was the knightliest soul and the truest gentleman I ever met."

On account of Frémont's services in opening the way across the continent to the Pacific coast, his admirers gave him at an early day the significant title of "The Pathfinder." After his failure in Missouri and his removal from the command of the army in that state, several of his brother officers presented him with an elegant sword as a testimonial of their regard. On one side of the sword this inscription was engraved: "To the Pathfinder, by the Men of the West."

In the history of our country John C. Frémont will continue to be remembered, not for his military achievements nor for his political aspirations, but

because he was the true pathfinder to the distant
West, carrying the nation's flag across the great
mountains and helping to extend our country's
boundaries to the Pacific coast.

THE STORY OF
ELISHA KENT KANE

ELISHA KENT KANE

ELISHA KENT KANE

CHAPTER I

BOYHOOD

What kind of boy do you suppose is reqired to become a man that can force his way through frozen seas, and travel over lands covered with mountains of ice and snow? He must not be afraid of the dark, for in those lands he must live for months without seeing daylight. He must not be afraid of cold, for he must often sleep out of doors with the mercury many degrees below zero, eat frozen food, and drink melted snow. He must not be afraid of wild animals, for he must hunt foxes and bears and seals and walruses. He must not be afraid of work, for he must often toil all day and all night, with no time to rest. He must not be afraid of study, for he must be able to measure mountains, calculate distances, observe the stars, and write about the heavens and the earth. He must not be careless and unkind, for he is responsible for the lives and spirits of the men in his party, even when they are ill and troublesome. In short, he must be brave, healthy, industrious, and learned, if he would undertake such journeys and accomplish them successfully.

Elisha Kent Kane was just the boy to become such a man. Although he was not always so willing to study as it was thought he should be, and although he was not so strong as one could wish, still he was so brave and fearless and persistent that he did much more when he grew up than most men do who have better health.

He was born February 3, 1820, in Philadelphia, and "went through the diseases and the training of infancy vigorously, with that energy of nerve and that sort of twill in the muscular texture which give tight little fellows more size than they measure and more weight than they weigh."

Elisha Kane was never large nor strong, but neither did he allow his smallness of size nor his lack of strength to interfere with anything that he undertook. He came of ancestors who loved their country and sacrificed themselves for it without any pay, and he nobly followed their fine example.

He was bold and daring, and always willing to

help any one in trouble, especially his younger brothers and sisters. There was no hill too high for him to climb, no difficulty too great for him to undertake, and no risk too heavy for him to run if there was some object to be attained, no matter how foolish that object might be.

One day he made up his mind to climb the kitchen chimney. It was sixteen feet high. How could he do it? Night came. With his little brother Tom, he descended from their bedroom window to the kitchen roof. Here he had hidden a clothesline with a stone tied at one end. He threw the stone again and again, until it fell into the chimney and rattled down to the room below.

Slipping through the skylight into this room, he fastened the end of the rope; then he clambered back to the roof and gave the slack rope to Tom, who was to keep it from swinging out over the ground. Up Elisha climbed, with his feet against the chimney and his hands clinging to the rope. The top of the chimney was touched, but how could he get up there?

He took hold of the edge, but the brick loosened in his hand. Throwing his arm over into the black chimney, he succeeded in pulling himself up, and called out to the boy below, "Oh,

Tom, what a nice place this is! I'll get down into the flue to my waist and pull you up, too. Just make a loop in the rope and I'll haul you up. Don't be afraid; it is grand up here."

But Elisha was not quite strong enough for that, and Tom never climbed the chimney. I wonder if Elisha ever thought of this when years afterward he climbed glaciers, threw ropes about an iceberg, or dropped into the crater of a volcano.

CHAPTER II

STUDIES MEDICINE

I am afraid his poor mother had a hard time trying to train this wild boy; his teachers certainly had. But those were days when the subjects a boy was required to study were not always the subjects best for him. Elisha made observations of the weather and the stars, rode horseback, drew maps of the country, secured collections of minerals, and worked away at chemistry with all the interest in the world. In his spare time he read " Robinson Crusoe" and " Pilgrim's Progress."

When Elisha Kane was thirteen years old, his father, who was a close student and an elegant and accomplished gentleman, said that all this nonsense must cease, and that his son must prepare for college.

For two or three years the boy made a brave effort to study, and then went to Yale College for examination.

He had not been well enough prepared in some branches to enter Yale, and was finally taken to the University of Virginia, where he could pursue the studies he liked best. These studies were science and mathematics.

Here he worked faithfully till he was eighteen, when he was taken violently ill, and went home expecting to die. His fine constitution carried him through, however, and after months of suffering he began to recover.

When his physician told him that he would probably never be strong again, he said he had "determined to make his mark in the world, and to die in the harness." After his illness he seemed to have lost his trying habits and characteristics, and he became "sedate, earnest, calm, and gentle."

As soon as his strength returned he began the study of medicine, and when only nineteen was hard at work in a hospital. There he made a brilliant record, and led his class; but at his father's wish he soon afterward entered the navy as surgeon, and was sent at once to China. This was in 1843, when Mr. Frémont was in the midst of his discoveries and explorations in the Far West.

Dr. Kane was always seasick on shipboard, but he studied just as hard as if he were well, and when the ship touched at any port he was up and away, scouring the country in every direction and learning about the people and their customs. His ship companions said that by the time they were ready to start out for a bit of sight-seeing he was usually on his way back to the ship.

He hunted elephants in Ceylon, explored the cave temples of Bombay, traveled extensively in China, and made a close study of the Philippine Islands.

An interesting story is told of his descent into the crater of a great volcano. He and Baron Loë started together, but the baron became alarmed, gave up the plan, and did his best to persuade Dr. Kane to do the same. Even the servants objected; but they finally gathered some bamboo sticks and made a kind of rope by which they let Dr. Kane over a precipice into the crater. Down he slid two hundred feet, and then unfastening the bamboo rope, clambered still lower to the smoking lake at the bottom. He filled some bottles with the bubbling liquid and then he tried to scramble back. But this was hard work, for the burning ashes slipped from under his feet, and the fumes of sulphur almost strangled him. His shoes were burned off, and he had barely strength to fasten the rope about his waist and give the signal to the men above. When he was drawn out the men found that he had fainted.

The natives said he had angered the god of the volcano, who was punishing him, and they undertook to complete this punishment by trying to kill him. A stray shot or two from Dr. Kane's revolver made them decide to leave the matter to the god of the volcano to settle.

Fifteen months after leaving home the ship on which Dr. Kane had sailed returned to America, but the young physician was not on board. He had decided to stay in China until he had earned enough money by his profession to travel extensively.

Six months later he was very sick with a fever, and when he recovered he felt obliged to start for home. Traveling with an invalid friend, he proceeded slowly to Singapore, across the Bay of

Bengal to Ceylon, and thence to the Indian Pe-
ninsula. For months the two companions toured
in India, climbing mountains and making friends
with the native princes.

With his friend's consent, Dr. Kane finally
joined the suite of an Indian prince, who was
about to make a visit to Queen Victoria. They
traveled together as far as Alexandria, but in
April, 1845, Dr. Kane said good-by to the prince,
who went to England alone, while the doctor made
a journey up the Nile, with a little American flag
at the head of his boat.

CHAPTER III

IN FOREIGN LANDS

We know very little about these months of
Egyptian travel, for Dr. Kane left few notes. In
a letter he says: "My Thebes life is a very wild
one. I am in native dress, with a beard so long
that I have to tuck it in. My lodging is on the
hot ground, and I walk on an average twenty-six
miles a day."

One night he lay down to sleep on the sand.
His boat was drawn up beside him, and his ser-

vant was lying on top of the boat with the trunks and baggage. When Dr. Kane awoke, everything was gone. He thought a quicksand had swallowed up his outfit, but when he found the boat two miles down the river, and discovered his watch chain around the neck of a man who was carrying him ashore, he changed his mind, ducked' the thief in the water, and after a hard fight secured the watch and chain.

Although he had lost nearly everything he owned, Dr. Kane did not leave Egypt, but continued his journey. One day he decided to climb the sitting statue of Memnon. This statue was many times as high as the old kitchen chimney, but he started up, determined to see what was inscribed on the tablet that lies on the knees of the statue.

The only way he could reach this tablet was by climbing up one leg of the statue, bracing his back or neck against the other leg. When he reached the tablet, he could not climb upon it, neither could he climb down. There he hung, back down, till an Arab horseman galloped over the sand and found a guide who knew the way up the back of the statue. A little later the Arab's dangling sash swung out over the edge of the tablet. Dr. Kane caught the end of the sash, let himself drop, swung out into the air, and was pulled safely up by the guide. He then walked quietly down by the usual way.

Soon after this adventure he went to Greece, where he walked from one interesting ruin to another, growing stronger slowly, until he had explored Greece from one end to the other. Thence he crossed the Adriatic Sea to Trieste, and passed on to Germany and Switzerland.

He seemed to find the ice and glaciers of the Alps most interesting. He examined them so carefully that the records which he made of his observations proved to be genuine additions to scientific knowledge.

We next find him in Paris, where he tried to secure a license from Spain to go to the island of Luzon, in the Philippines, and practice his profession. Spain would not give him this license, and he soon passed over into Italy, through France to England, and finally home to America.

A few months later, when our war with Mexico was beginning, Dr. Kane begged to be sent there for active service; but much to his disappointment, he was ordered to Africa instead.

On the 25th of May, 1846, he sailed away to

make a study of the conditions of slavery in Africa. He visited the king of Dahomey in his own king- dom. This Dahomeyan king had a courtyard covered with the skulls of the men he had killed with his saber. He offered to kill a few subjects to entertain his visitor, but Dr. Kane persuaded him not to do this. He concluded from what he saw that perhaps the slave trade did not seem so dreadful to these poor creatures as it did to him.

On his way back to America, Dr. Kane fell severely ill of coast fever. He was sent directly to his home, where he struggled back to life, though he never fully recovered from the effects of his journey to the hot, unhealthful African coast.

CHAPTER IV

IN MEXICO

Dr. Kane was very much in earnest about go- ing to Mexico. As soon as he was able to travel, he hurried to Washington to ask again to be sent out in the Mexican service. There he was again taken sick, but on his recovery his earnest wish was rewarded, and he was sent to Mexico.

He carried important dispatches, and was directed to visit and report upon the hospital service in the United States Army stationed in Mexico.

In November he left Philadelphia, taking with him a beautiful Kentucky horse. From New Orleans the steamer "Fashion" carried him to Vera Cruz, but not without danger, for in a heavy storm the ship seemed breaking in pieces. There were many horses on board, and one by one they were backed into the ocean; but Dr. Kane's favorite horse was spared.

The storm grew heavier; all hands were bailing out water with camp kettles, for the pumps were broken. Then unexpectedly the ship was driven into port, and the crew experienced what seemed to be a miraculous escape.

A regiment was leaving Vera Cruz for the city of Mexico, and Dr. Kane joined it; but at an inland town he decided to join a "renegade spy company," and to proceed with them, thinking thus to arrive more quickly.

While he was in this questionable company, the party came suddenly upon a band of Mexican guerrillas, accompanied by several generals and men of note. In the battle which followed, Dr.

Kane was the leading spirit. His party was victorious, but the men, who were almost savages, set upon and were killing their prisoners. Kane interfered and ordered them to stop, enforcing his orders with his six-shooter. The prisoners were spared, and frankly said they owed their lives to Dr. Kane.

The gallant Kentucky horse had been killed in the fight, and Dr. Kane himself was severely wounded. Forgetting his own sufferings, he helped those who were wounded till he fell in a faint. He was carried to the home of a Mexican general, whose son's life he had just saved by a surgical operation. There he was tenderly cared for by the general's own family, and Dr. Kane in turn owed his life to them.

Weak and useless, he was ordered home, and his transportation papers were made out; but he refused to go, saying: "Mexico I will not leave until I can do so clearly—until the armistice is more definite or peace is more prospective."

The armistice was arranged and he was finally persuaded to go home. He writes: "My leave is but for three weeks; my object a surgical operation; my health such as to require all the kindly care of the home to which I again return, a broken-down man. My hair would be gray but that I have no hair. My hopes would be particularly small but that I have no hopes."

CHAPTER V

SENT TO THE ARCTIC SEAS

In 1849 Dr. Kane made a voyage to Lisbon and Rio Janeiro, from which he returned, ill and emaciated, to a quiet station on Mobile Bay in Alabama. Here, by the shores of the Gulf of Mexico, he was growing strong and doing some surveying for the government, when one day a short, sharp summons came from Washington—a telegram which read, "Proceed at once to New York for duty on the Arctic expedition."

Without delay he thrust his belongings into a satchel, and hastened to New York by the quickest route. After a few hours of preparation in that city he embarked and was soon on his way to Polar waters.

Why was he going?

One of the most daring and successful of Arctic explorers had been Sir John Franklin. He had made four voyages in search of the North Pole—

SIR JOHN FRANKLIN

the first in 1818, the second in 1819, the third in 1825, and the fourth in 1845. Since 1845 nothing had been heard from him, although fifteen different expeditions had been sent from England to search for the missing men and ships. Poor Lady Franklin had begged her own countrymen as well as Americans to go once more to his relief. Henry Grinnell, of New York, offered to furnish two small brigs for such a search if men could be found to undertake the journey. The Secretary of the Navy detailed men in the service, with instruments and rations for a three years' cruise. Lieutenant De Haven was put in charge, and Dr. Kane was appointed surgeon.

On the 22d of May, 1850, the poor-looking little vessels, the "Advance" and the "Rescue," sailed out of New York Bay. Although small and rather low, they proved to be well fitted for their work; for ships that must hammer their way through fields of ice and underneath huge overhanging icebergs must be small, but strong.

These vessels were built double, like one boat inside another, while the hull was wedge-shaped. The hull was built in this shape so that when "nipped" by the ice it would be lifted, and not crushed. The decks were double, and packed be-

HENRY GRINNELL

tween with tarred felt.   The inside was lined with cork, which made it dry and warm.   Extra beams in all directions braced the sides, and the rudder was so built that it could be taken off if the ice became too troublesome.   A great funnel was put about the stovepipe in the cabin, so that snow could be melted for water.   There were also a blacksmith's forge, stoves, and extra boats on board.   All these things had been furnished by Mr. Grinnell.

The government supplied the guns, ammunition, and instruments, and these, I am sorry to say, were very poor.   The guns were old-fashioned and out of order, and the instruments were by no means the best.

The men, twenty-three in number, were not well, nor had they had experience in such travel; but they proved willing and true.

When these little vessels sailed out of New York harbor there was no government salute, but the wharves and the rigging of the ships at anchor were black with people who cheered themselves hoarse to honor these men who were risking their lives for the sake of others.   Mr. Grinnell and his sons, on a fine pilot boat, kept them company till the next day, when they hoisted a white flag, signaled good-by, and returned to New York.

After their friends were gone, all hands turned in to arrange the small cabins. Each man had a berth to himself. This was a space six feet long by three feet wide and three feet high. Into such a space Dr. Kane crawled with a box of tacks and some India-rubber cloth. He covered the inside of his berth with the cloth to keep out the wet, and spread his Astrachan fur cloak with some other skins on the bottom for a bed. He hung his watch on one nail, his ink bottle on another, and a thermometer on a third. He put up two little shelves for his books, while his tooth-brush, comb, and hair-brush were hung from a string. At the head of the berth was a shelf with a lamp on it. These quarters were to be his home for fifteen months.

When the work was all done, he said: "I crawled in from the wet and cold through a slit in the India-rubber cloth, and it would be hard for any one to realize the quantity of comfort which I felt I had manufactured." The lamp was bright, the furs were warm, and he was at home.

CHAPTER VI

IN THE POLAR REGIONS

Now, though Dr. Kane says nothing about it, he was really very ill, and when the brigs reached Greenland Lieutenant De Haven tried to send him home; but the doctor flatly refused to be sent. · He was full of excitement and enthusiasm. Icebergs as large as great buildings began to loom up on all sides, whales were seen, and soon Greenland, a country without a sign of green, but covered with ice and snow, lay full in sight.

They were now so far north that the sun was above the horizon from two in the morning till ten at night, and the men found it very hard to go to sleep. By June 24th there was no night at all. The sun did not drop below the horizon, though the days were not always bright. There were fogs and pale sunshine and cold drizzling rain, while icebergs sparkling in the sun or lying deep in shadow were their constant companions.

It was hard to keep up the regular routine of the ship's work, but the commander knew that it must be done. The men were called early in the morning, and washed themselves in their "one tin wash-basin." After breakfast they worked, and played games; after dinner they went for a walk or a hunt over the ice; after supper they went to bed as regularly as at home.

Their first stop was made at the Crown Prince Islands. It was raining. The harbor was guarded on both sides by huge rocks covered with ice, down which trickled streams of water. There were no trees nor houses nor people in sight. Presently they saw a poor old building, and a "something like a large Newfoundland dog moving rapidly through the water." This "something" was a Greenlander in a kayak, which is a queer boat built in a curious way. A framework like a canoe is covered with skins, top and sides and bottom. A small hole is left in the middle, around which is a stiff rim. The Greenlander sits down in this opening and pulls the bottom of his sealskin jumper (which is water-tight at neck and wrist) over the stiff rim. In this way he is really sitting in a tight skin bag, so built that it rides the water like a cork.

The Greenlanders love these strange little boats, and do wonderful things in them. As long as a rock or a piece of ice does not cut the skin, nothing can harm the fisherman; but a very small hole will send him to instant death, and such deaths are not uncommon.

Soon crowds of these boats were bobbing after the ships, sometimes under water, sometimes

AN ESKIMO AND HIS HUT

above it, and rapidly propelled by a short, double-headed oar. After a little the people on shore were seen; there were forty of them crowded to-gether, noisy, dirty, and shouting with excitement. The rocks were covered with pieces of meat, spread out to dry in the sun, and everything was coated with grease and filth.

Near by were the Eskimo huts. These huts are all built much alike. Large pieces of rock or turf or ice form the sides, while bones are used to hold up a roof of the same materials. A little square hole is cut for a window, and the opening is covered with the thin intestine of a seal, for the Eskimos have no glass. The entrance is made through a kind of tunnel several feet long, but only large enough for one person at a time to crawl through on hands and knees. The opening to this tunnel is covered with heavy skins.

The first thing one would see, when once inside, would probably be a pile of blocks of ice, to be melted for drinking water. A raised platform runs around the wall, and on this platform is the lamp which is used for heating and cooking. On this same platform the entire family piles itself up to sleep or eat. On one such platform, in a hut six by eight feet square, Dr. Kane found a "father, mother, grandfather, four children, a tea-kettle, box, two rifles, and a litter of puppies."

The Eskimos have a few bone dishes with a stone bowl for melting snow, and a bowl or two of sealskin, which are used for all purposes and never washed. The walls are usually dripping wet, black with smoke and grease, and covered with mold. Here the women tend the smoking lamps, make the skin clothes, and do the cooking.

Much of their food is eaten raw, for the men do not go out on the hunt until they are nearly starved; and when the food is brought in no one waits for it to be cooked. All the family sit down on the ground, and cutting strips from the frozen seal or walrus, throw back their heads, swallow as much as they can at one time, and cut off the end close to the mouth; then they cut off another strip and devour that. The babies have their own knives, and eat as long as the older people. The men often eat as much as eight or ten pounds of meat at a time, then roll over and go to sleep, waking only to reach out for more meat, and then to go to sleep again.

Their sandwiches are made of two slices of frozen seal meat with a chunk of blubber between. Sometimes they have birds to eat. The hunter goes out with a net fastened to a long pole, and lying on the ground easily nets the birds. Then he bites their heads to kill them, or links their wings together if he wishes to keep them alive, and throws them into a bag made of his

skin jumper with its sleeves tied together. These
birds are afterwards cut open and frozen, or left
lying in a heap, to be used when wanted. Dr. Kane
says he once heard an Eskimo baby cry out in the
night that it was cold. The mother sat up, reached
out and picked up a couple of birds, killed and
skinned them, and drew the warm skins over the
baby's cold feet.

CHAPTER VII

FAST IN THE ICE

All this time we have left Lieutenant De Haven
at anchor at the Crown Prince Islands, although
he was eager to get away. He had heard of the
passing of some English vessels, bound on the
same errand as his own, and longed to be moving
toward the north. He bought all the furs he
could, and sent Dr. Kane to Lively for more,
while he awaited the arrival of the companion
brig, the "Rescue."

Dr. Kane made his trip in a small boat through
water so clear that wonderful growths of seaweed
could be seen far below. At Lively he went to
the quaint home of the "Royal Inspector of the

Northern Portions of Davis Straits." This man was well educated, but lived a very hard life in that forbidding place. It was his business to go from one poor group of Eskimo huts to another, on a sledge drawn by dogs. He must preserve peace among the natives, collect furs, and keep all reminded that they were subjects of the Danish government.

The Royal Inspector and his assistant not only received Dr. Kane most kindly, but almost robbed themselves to supply his needs. The furs bought here were made into Eskimo suits for the men. Each suit consisted of a pair of boots and a "jumper." The boots were without seams, and reached above the hips. The jumper was a fur shirt made with a hood, and reached below the tops of the boots.

When the "Advance" and "Rescue" left the Crown Prince Islands they were well equipped for their hard work in the ice-fields. As the little vessels scudded out of the harbor the men laughed to think how carefully they had avoided each bit of ice on their way up from New York. Now, indeed, there was ice to be avoided—great floating fields of it, surging and thrashing about them, and tossing huge masses of slush and great cakes of ice upon greater masses beneath, while icebergs, like towered castles, floated slowly by.

The noise and tumult of the floating ice were deafening and terrible, not at all the quiet place one would imagine a sea of ice to be. The icebergs crowded past more and more thickly, and while the people of New York were sending up their Fourth-of-July skyrockets, and trying to cool themselves with ice cream, the little vessels were surrounded by two hundred and forty icebergs, and the crews had no fear of sunstroke.

Day by day the explorers cruised along at the edge of this frozen sea, breaking through the long tongues of ice that ran out into the clear water, and always keeping the vessels headed north. But before long they were not skirting along the edge of the ice, but were entirely surrounded by it. The stout little vessels were bumped and whirled and lifted and dropped and forced backward and plunged forward by the great masses of ice.

They kept their noses pointed through the slush and floating chunks, persistently breaking through the young ice as it formed. But one morning, in spite of all their efforts, Dr. Kane was forced to write in his journal: " Fast! Around us a circle of snow-covered ice streaked with puddles

of dark water, and varied by the very distant loom-
ing of some icebergs.   In the center of this drear-
iness are the two vessels, the 'Advance' and the
' Rescue.' "

Lieutenant De Haven hoped he could bore his
way out, and the man aloft kept anxious watch for
openings, or "leads," in the field of ice.   As soon
as one appeared, the boat would be headed toward
it, while every one held his breath.   " De Haven
shouts, ' Hard-a-starboard!'   The brig urges her
nose into a sudden indentation and bangs her
quarter against a big lump of swashing ice.
'Steady there!'—a second yell—'Down, down!
Hard down!'   And then we rub and scrape and
jam and thrust aside and are thrust aside."   They
manage to enter the crack, or "lead," when suddenly they find the open space growing very narrow.   There are quick orders shouted, " ' Helm-a-
starboard! Port! Easy! So! Steadie-ee-ee! Hard-
a-port, hard, hard, hard!' (Scrape, scratch, thump.)
And we are jammed fast between two great ice-
fields of unknown extent."   Nothing can be done,
and so the captain comes down and the crew goes
to supper.

Sometimes they tried to use the boat as a
wedge.   Men were sent, leaping over the ice, to

place an anchor, adjust the ropes, and with a hearty pull force the boat farther into the narrow crack. Sometimes the crack opened, and the boats would advance a few feet, drawn by the willing men; but their efforts were useless. At the end of three weeks they had advanced only a few feet, and were slowly swinging about in the great ice-pack, helpless and motionless.

CHAPTER VIII

BEARS AND WALRUSES

As the vessels lay imprisoned in the ice, the men began to think of hunting. Seals were sometimes seen, and the men tried hard to catch them. These strange animals looked so much like Eskimos that the men could hardly tell them apart. The natives hunted them in a queer way, and by watching them, the white men soon learned how they did it. They would crouch down behind a screen made of skin or cloth, and creep along over the ice until near enough to shoot the animal before he knew an enemy was in sight.

The yellowish white polar bears stalked majestically across the ice, dragging their great feet in a slow and heavy swing. Often these huge fellows came close up to the vessel, because they did not know enough to be afraid. The men would rush below for their guns, shouting, "Bear, bear!"

SHOOTING SEALS

But one or two shots had no effect, and the great bears would lumber off unhurt.

These bears became very annoying, for they would break up the caches which the men had carefully built. The caches were made by piling kegs and cans of meat, coffee, and other supplies

on the ice.   Large stones and blocks of ice were
heaped over them, and water poured over all to
freeze and make a solid hill of preserved food.

The bears would find these caches, tear them

ESKIMO HUNTING THE POLAR BEAR

to pieces, smash the kegs and cans, and eat up the
food.   They did not like salt meat, but cleared
up all the coffee, swallowed the American flag,
chewed the rubber cloth, and tied it full of knots,
played foot-ball with the kegs, and added insult to
injury by sliding down the hill on their haunches.

One old mother bear led the men and dogs a long chase. The dogs were worrying her, snapping at her heels and jumping at her head. She would catch up her baby, which was with her, throw it ahead of her on the ice, face the dogs, and fight them off until she backed up to where the cub lay; then she would pick it up, throw it ahead again, and so proceed until she had led the dogs a long way from the hunters. But the baby grew tired. Then the old mother bear reared herself up on her hind legs, put the baby bear between them, and began to growl, showing her teeth, and striking furiously at the dogs with her front paws. When the hunters caught up with the bear they shot her dead. Then the baby bear jumped up on the mother's body and put up a grand fight for its own life, but was finally shot and killed, cached, and left until the men could return.

The polar bears are terrible fighters, and as hard to kill as the grizzly bear. Their meat when cooked tastes as if soaked in lamp oil.

Sometimes the explorers killed a walrus. These great animals always had one of their number act as a sentinel while the rest slept. Sometimes a mother walrus would be seen with her two babies. If the men tried to kill them the mother walrus would

catch up her babies, throw them into the water,
jump in after them, catch them in her arms, and
dive out of sight.

Walruses are very dangerous animals. Some-

HUNTING THE WALRUS

times they attack a boat full of men. A story is
told of such a fight. Just as the men were afraid
the walruses had beaten them, one walrus put his
head over the side of the boat. A man shoved his
rifle into his throat and fired. The great animal

fell back dead, and the walrus's comrades carried him away on their tusks.

An Eskimo hunter must be very strong and active to capture such huge beasts. He creeps up on the ice until near enough to hurl a harpoon into his body. A strong walrus-skin rope is fastened to the harpoon. The walrus plunges into the water, but he cannot get away, for the rope holds him fast. Slowly drawing in the rope as the beast gives him a chance, the hunter at length gets near enough to deal the death-blow. Then the body is divided among all the hunters, the one who killed the walrus getting the best cuts.

CHAPTER IX

TRACES OF FRANKLIN

All this while our friends have been fast in the ice, doing their best to occupy the time with hunts and games, with races and hard work, until one joyful day in July the ice suddenly opened, and the ships were once more afloat. They passed near cliffs of red snow. One man dug down for several feet into this strange snow, and found it always the same dull deep red. Dr. Kane examined some which was red to the depth of about eight inches.

Of course, there were no large trees or shrubs as we know them, but only poor, crawling, scraggly things lying close to the rocks. There were trees no higher than one's shoes, but perfect in form. Vines which at home grew large enough to cover a porch, here were only large enough for a buttonhole, while willow trees were the size of a clover.

The Arctic summer was fast slipping away, and our explorers had found no sign of Dr. Franklin's party, although they had kept up an earnest search. One day they came in sight of a cairn on the land with a flagstaff placed above it. An English vessel which had passed them had found sure traces of Franklin's party, and the excitement was intense.

Quickly landing, the explorers found signs of a camping place of a large party. There were bits of cloth and painted wood, and traces of camp fires where pieces of bone would seem to show that something had been cooked. These were slight traces and very discouraging, for there was no message nor sign of where the travelers had gone.

Just at this time they found that Captain

Penny, commander of one of the English vessels, had made a most important discovery. A short distance from the first camp his men had found a tin can stamped with the name of the London manufacturer who had put up food for Franklin's party. Then there was a scrap of a newspaper with the date 1845 upon it. There were other bits of paper also, on one of which was the name of one of Franklin's officers. A scrap of a stocking and a pocket from an English officer's coat were also found. It looked as if there might have been a shipwreck, or as if a party were moving slowly along. Strangely enough, five of the vessels carrying search parties were now collected in this one spot eagerly examining the ice in all directions.

The officers were earnestly consulting and making plans for a systematic search, when a man came rushing over the ice shouting, "Graves, Captain Penny! graves! graves! Franklin's winter quarters!"

Everybody rushed over the rough, crumbling ice. A hard scramble of several miles brought them in sight of three boards shaped like gravestones standing at the head of three graves. On the boards were cut the names and ages of the men who had died. Near by were bits of iron and nails, and a piece of wood which had been used for an anvil. Not far away were more than six hundred meat cans filled with stones. There were all kinds of pieces of rope, matches, cloth, wood, iron, clothing, and paper. They even found traces of a sledge, and near by, a little Arctic garden. There was no sign of where the party had gone or of what was their condition. This baffling silence was almost harder to bear than if nothing at all had been discovered.

Two more English vessels soon joined them, and one· notable day there were eight different expeditions collected at this one point, all bent on the same humane errand. What seems still more strange is, that after going their separate ways these eight vessels met again three weeks later, although they had not seen each other in the mean time, and had been buffeted by ice and beaten by storms for many days.

It was now late in September, and Lieutenant De Haven feeling that the season's work must close, and having had orders not to remain in the Arctic regions if it could be avoided, now headed for home. Days of awful struggle and exposure followed. Flung about by gales, hurled high by plunging ice-floats, scudding before the wind, or being towed more slowly by some huge iceberg, the explorers passed many anxious days. Once it seemed as if their fate was sealed; the vessels were fast in the ice. After days of waiting, supplies were transferred to the ice and plans formed for winter quarters. Suddenly, with a deafening crash, the ice broke away, and they were afloat, leaving part of their stores behind them on the ice.

Again they were fast in a great cake of ice, drifting helplessly among tumbling mountains of water and slush, which pitched the ships in every direction, lifting them bodily from the water, packing huge cakes of ice beneath them, then suddenly sliding them back into the churning water. This terrible strain lasted more than two months, when they were finally forced to admit that they must remain where they were till the next September.

Slowly and sadly they put the "Advance" into winter trim. A heavy jacket of felt was drawn over the deck, covering it as closely as possible from the cold. Each man's baggage was packed, so that in case the ships should be crushed all hands could escape, carrying their most precious belongings with them.

There were strange, dull exhibitions of the aurora borealis, which was all they had to lighten the dreadful darkness of the Arctic winter. The cold grew more intense. The water casks in the cabin froze up, a cup of water froze solid in five minutes; everything they touched burned the bare hand like hot iron. The hatchway was so full of icicles that a new entrance had to be made to the cabin.

Wrought iron became as brittle as glass, dried apples froze solid in the barrels, and were chopped up, barrel and all, and carried down below. The sugar had to be sawed up into chunks; butter was cut with a chisel and mallet; the meat was mined with a crowbar; and a barrel of oil, from which the barrel had been broken, stood all winter, a yellow, cylindrical mass. The meat as it came from the cans could have been used for cannon balls.

If they wished an ice for dessert after a meal of these delightful things, they poured a little boiling water over some cranberries and sugar and butter, and it was ready. To be sure, the spoon froze to their mouths, unless they were careful, and took away the skin as part of the second spoonful. Out of doors one's breath looked as if a pistol had been fired from his mouth; icicles hung from the men's mustaches; if they talked, their tongues froze to their lips. Sometimes their eyes froze shut; and if they touched their faces with their gloves, a knife was needed to cut them loose again.

CHAPTER X

WINTER IN THE ICE

And so the slow, dark months dragged by. The men grew deadly white. Some were ill, then more were ill, and finally all were ill. The doctor worked continuously. The men tried hard to fight down disease, and to keep up courage, but this was a hard thing to do when they were drifting helplessly in ice, no one knew where.

Dr. Kane says that when the bell rang to get up, for there was no morning, he would sit up and drink a glass of water, "eyes and nose and mouth chippy with lampblack." Next he bathed himself in snow slush, and rubbed himself dry with a hard towel. After that he put on his queer fur clothes, and ate a breakfast of griddle cakes and mackerel. Then followed a climb over the ice and snow, a little study, a game of football, or a hunt.

After dinner the men sometimes washed their bedding in pulverized snow, and passed the dreadful afternoon in the horrid-smelling cabin, and then turned in for the night.

These months of darkness were only a struggle to keep alive, and as free as possible from the loathsome illnesses which poor food and no daylight bring to men. Sometimes there were plays given in the long hours after dinner. The deck was the theater, and kegs were the opera chairs. The theater was not a warm one, for the thermometer often ranged from six to forty-six degrees below zero.

Of course the men took all the different parts, and it was very amusing to see a great six-foot man act the part of a delicate young girl. With his long whiskers and heavy boots, and singing a song in a deep bass voice, and in an Irish brogue, he made a very queer-appearing girl. The performers moved in a mist so thick that the audience could scarcely see them. Their hands steamed and their breath came in clouds. If one took off his hat, "his head smoked like a dish of potatoes."

They tried to be very merry on Christmas with such a play, using a jew's-harp for an orchestra, and giving each other cakes of soap for Christmas gifts. Old songs and older stories served to keep the dinner table in a roar.

The year 1850 closed with a shout of joy from the men, for at noonday it was light enough out of doors to read large print. Early in March there came a break in the ice, which gave a glimpse of hope to all the men. Even the sick men more willingly swallowed the doses of oil and lime juice, or scraped raw potatoes and sauer-kraut mixed with molasses, for there was now some inducement to wish to live.

The ice soon began to grumble with noises like "the grating of nutmegs or humming of bees or yapping of puppies." These were sure signs of the breaking up which must soon follow.

In April the weather seemed warm at zero; the felt covering was stripped from the brig, the smoky lamps were cleaned, the cabin opened to the light of day, and the lampblack-covered clothes hung out to air. The frozen blankets were thawed and dried, and the blessed daylight allowed to fill every corner of the reeking cabin. The men fell gayly to work making new sealskin clothes and snow-goggles, for the daylight had brought a new trouble—snow-blindness. These goggles were round pieces of wood with narrow slits cut in them, and served their purpose better than glass goggles.

CHAPTER XI

OFF FOR HOME

All through the winter the little brig "Rescue" had been ice-bound only a few feet from the "Advance." Her officers had, however, lived on board the "Advance," because the smaller vessel was in greater danger of being crushed by the ice. In June there was a joyful shout: "Ice cracking ahead!" The "Rescue's" officers leaped from the "Advance," sprang across a narrow crack (a ribbon of water which was almost instantly a river), shouting: "Stick by the floe; good-by; what news for home?" And they were off.

All was confusion, the ice was splitting in all directions, the noise was deafening. At length the "Advance" was free, except for a great piece of ice almost as large as herself which stuck to her stern. A few days later she was freed from this burden, and started at once in the track of the " Rescue," headed for the settlements of Greenland.

Although the voyage was far from easy, they finally landed at Pröven. The Danish governor and his family gave them a hearty welcome. The governor's family, as well as four generations of his wife's family, lived in a one-roomed house, 15 by 16 feet in size. The ceiling was just high enough to allow a man to stand erect. The room was furnished much like the Eskimo huts. A shelf was built around the wall, and on it dogs, people, babies, birds, dishes, clothes, and food were heaped together, without any regard to order. In spite of this the family were happy, good-natured, and hospitable.

For the second time in their lives our explorers celebrated the Fourth of July in a cool place. They rolled huge stones down the cliffs, which made a noise louder than any fire-crackers or a cannon. They ate and drank as if it were a holiday at home.

One day an English whaling vessel called at the port and gave our party a generous present of newspapers, turnips, potatoes, eggs, and fresh beef. While these were things they had not seen for many months, they almost forgot them in their delight at the sight of English faces and the sound of the English language.

Proceeding to Upernavik, they were given another warm welcome by the governor there, and felt that they were once more in touch with their own world.

The governor of Upernavik lived in a very odd house with a high gable and a red roof. Two other houses and a steepled church made the port seem like a city to the men. When they saw the governor's garden their delight was boundless. This garden was ten feet square and covered with glass! By scraping away the frost from the glass one could see real radishes and turnip tops beneath!

The governor's daughters, in dresses made of cloth, tried hard to entertain the men. They could not understand the English language, but their knowledge of the common courtesies of life was a perfect joy to men who had not seen a home for more than a year. They hardly knew how to act when they saw the supper table covered with a white cloth and bearing clean dishes filled with coffee, eggs, and brown bread. And when on their return trip, as a crowning act of hospitality, ten radishes were brought in "on the bottom of a blue saucer—crisp, pale, yet blushing at their tips," the men thought them food fit for the gods.

After days of refitting, cheered by letters from home, which the men sat up all night to read, the ships' prows were again turned toward the north. The summer was now full upon them, and if anything was to be done it must be done at once. But August found them still aimlessly floating, waiting for a break in the pack ice, which never came, and so they reluctantly turned toward home. They called upon their friends at Upernavik, and in September found themselves once more in New York harbor, where Mr. Grinnell was the first to bid them welcome as they touched the wharf.

CHAPTER XII

PLANS FOR A NEW EXPEDITION

Sir John Franklin had not been found, and Dr. Kane believed there was still a chance for his life. He thought that, though shipwrecked, the party might have escaped to some settlement of Eskimos, where they were still awaiting deliverance.

Dr. Kane believed that there was an open polar sea, into which the Gulf Stream deposited the material it ever carries toward that dreary region, and where millions of birds nested and lived. He dreamed of it by night, while every day he was writing, lecturing, petitioning, bending every nerve toward the fitting out of a new expedition.

In December, 1852, the longed-for order came. Mr. Grinnell had put the "Advance" at his disposal; Mr. Peabody and other friends and organizations had furnished the outfit; and the Secretary of the Navy had detailed men, and supplied instruments for observations. Dr. Kane's plan was to sail as far north as possible, then to leave the brig and to continue the search by land, traveling on dog sledges. He thought there were animals enough for food, and that the Eskimos would help them in case they needed help.

Eighteen men were his companions, two of whom had been north before. From these men he exacted three things: first, there should be absolute obedience; second, no one should use liquor; third, there should be no swearing. Swiftly the sledges, tents, boards, clothes, knives, beads, books, instruments, and food were stowed away in the strong little "Advance." The preparations were quickly made, but not so carefully as they should have been for such a journey.

They sailed in May, 1853, hoping to reach a point very far north before winter came on. The governor at St. John's gave Dr. Kane a fine team of Newfoundland dogs, which, with the help of their Eskimo dogs, they hoped would carry them safely over the ice.

The Eskimo dogs were strange animals. They looked more like wolves than dogs, and were very wild and fierce. They would eat anything even, a feather bed. They ate a huge bird's-nest one day, "sticks, dirt, stones, moss, and all." They would not sleep in the dog-houses built for them, but lay close to the ship on the ice. Every day all the dogs would sit down in a circle on the ice and seem to hold an important consultation; they never barked.

When traveling, the dogs were fastened to a sledge by long leather thongs; the driver guided them by cracking a long whip. It took a great deal of practice to crack this whip close by the right dog. There were forty-one of these dogs in all. One was called Old Grim. He was always in sight when there was anything to eat, and always out of sight when there was anything

to do. One day the sledge was brought out. Old
Grim saw it and hid in a barrel. He was dragged
out, but suddenly pretended to be lame, and

AN ESKIMO DOG TEAM

always limped after that except when the team
was safely away on a journey. One day he was
tied with a rope and made to help on a sledge, but
he broke away, disappeared, and could never be
found again.

The Newfoundland dogs were noble fellows, and made all the trips within sixty miles of the ship. They were so strong they could draw very heavy loads, and when they fell ill they were taken into the cabin and cared for as if they were children. But it was of no use. All the Newfoundland dogs died, and all but six of the Eskimo dogs, before the winter was over.

CHAPTER XIII

JOURNEYING BY LAND AND SEA

The dog sledges used in the Arctic regions are most carefully built. The natives use bones for the framework, but Dr. Kane's men used wood fastened together with strips of sealskin. When the dogs were ill the men drew the sledges.

Each man had a "rueraddy"; this was a strap which passed over one shoulder and under the other arm, to which a long rope was fastened, and by which they drew the sledge. These ropes were of different lengths, so that the men could run behind one another.

Elaborate preparations were made for the first journeys from the ship. Tents, blankets, India-rubber cloth, camp kettles, and several kinds of food were loaded upon the sledges. But later on Dr. Kane carried only slabs of frozen meat for food, and a fur sleeping-bag for comfort.

In the meanwhile the "Advance" bumped her way through fields of ice, was fastened to and drawn by icebergs, passed the cliffs of crimson snow, weathered terrific gales, and proceeded in much the same manner as upon the former expedition. Winter began to close down early in September, and the explorers set to work on their winter quarters. They built an observatory of rocks, cemented with ice and frozen moss. They erected pedestals of snow and ice for their instruments, set their tide register, and built a house for their thermometers.

This little house was built of wood, bored full of holes, so the air could enter freely, while wooden screens were set up to keep out strong winds and drifting snow. A pane of glass was placed so that the thermometer could be read without going into the little house. These thermometers were so fine that if a man came near them the liquid in the tubes would instantly rise.

When everything was made snug, and before the winter's darkness settled upon them, Dr. Kane

planned to make many journeys from the ship,
carrying food to be cached on the ice in preparation for the great sledge journey to the far north
as soon as daylight should again come in the
spring. This plan was carried out as far as possible, but it was hard work. Trotting behind
sledges, urging on tired dogs, pulling the loads
out of water, sleeping in wet and frozen clothes,
going without fire to save alcohol, and without
food in order to leave enough at the caches—
such labors and trials were enough to kill the men.

One of the most terrible of these journeys was
made in March. The men had set off bravely,
cheering as they ran, and drawing a heavy sledge-
load of food to cache as far north as they could
possibly go. Upon their return the exploring and
searching party was to set out. Ten days later,
as the men on the brig were busily at work, three
of the brave party came in. They were suffering
horribly; their faces were swollen, their feet
frozen, and their minds wandering. They said
that the rest of the party were probably frozen to
death. They had been forced to leave them in the
drifting snow, and to return to the brig for help.

Some of the men flew for food, while others
prepared a sledge with food and furs, and laying

the least injured of the men on a sledge to act as guide, the relief party hurried to the rescue. Twenty-one hours later they saw a little American flag fluttering from a snow-drift. Under the snow-drift was the tent, and in the tent lay the men, frozen but still alive. How they cried when Dr. Kane and his party broke into the tent! They must be moved at once or die.

With the thermometer, seventy-five degrees below zero, the frozen men were sewed into bags of deerskin, and screaming with agony, were lifted upon the sledges. Then all set out for the brig, climbing over the hummocks or struggling around them as best they could. Strength failed; the cold was unbearable, and the men begged to sleep. Dr. Kane did all in his power to keep them awake; he struck them, made fun of them, and abused them; but sleep they would, even if it meant death. They were too cold to build a fire. Whisky which had been packed under all the furs was frozen to a lump of ice. But strangely enough this dreaded sleep refreshed them.

Dr. Kane and a man named Godfrey pushed on to the half-way tent to get some food ready for the rest of the party. In their absence the tent had been overturned by a bear. When it was finally raised again, the two men fell to the ground and slept for hours. Dr. Kane's whiskers froze to his sleeping-bag, and when he awoke he had to be cut loose. But the soup was ready for the others when they came up.

The men were rested by being allowed to sleep two minutes at a time in turn. Their thirst was horrible, and they were forced to eat snow. Their mouths swelled so they could not speak, and they were all delirious. No one seems to know how they reached the vessel, but they were all alive, though one was blind, and two had lost their toes. Two of them died two days later.

CHAPTER XIV

A VISIT FROM ESKIMOS

Almost as trying as these dreadful trips were the long days in the stuffy cabin, where in one tiny room the men cooked, ate, slept, sewed, made shoes, cared for the dogs, were ill, and even died. There was no daylight. In October the moon slowly swung around the entire horizon, shining clear and bright for many days, if one could call it day. When the moon was gone came darkness so deep that one could not count the fingers held before the face. For one hundred and forty-one days this lasted.

The time was filled in various ways. Obser-

MEETING THE ESKIMOS

vations were taken, keeping the hand covered with chamois skins so that it would not freeze to the instruments. Newspapers were written and read, plays enacted, games invented, and races run.

On the 21st of January the first tint of sunlight

appeared on the horizon, and by March there was too much day, just as there had before been too much night. Following De Haven's example, the hours were regularly assigned for work. The firewood was weighed daily, and the men worked hard to keep enough ice thawed to make drinking-water. The lamp oil was gone, and a bit of cotton pulled through a cork floating on a saucer of pork fat was their lamp. Food was frozen and becoming scarce.

The men were unable to walk, and must have fresh meat or die. There were no bears or seals, but an occasional fox could be caught. One poor little fellow had freed himself from his rock trap, but was frozen to the ground by his own breath and whiskers while burrowing his way to freedom. He made a fine supper for the hungry men.

One day the Eskimos appeared beside the brig. They had several dogs and sledges with them. They were not in the least afraid of the men, and laughed and talked while they stole whatever they could lay their hands on.

Some queer stories which these people told are very interesting. They said there once was an Eskimo woman who had some deformed children. She put these children into a shoe, and threw the shoe into the sea. The shoe grew into a ship, and the children became the white people, awful to see. They thought white cloth was the skin of these people, and that they lived on dry musk-ox meat.

The Eskimos tell this story of the sun and moon: The sun was once a lovely Eskimo girl, and the moon was her lover. During the long winter he came to see her. It was so dark she could not see who it was, for the lamp in the hut had gone out. She put her hand in the lampblack and touched his face. When the day came she found the man was her brother. She ran away; he followed her over land and sea. She sprang into the sky; he leaped after, and has been following her ever since. When the sun is eclipsed by the moon, they say the brother has caught his sister, and the lampblack is still on his face.

The Eskimo god is a man who lives in a great stone castle in the sea. This castle is very wonderful, and there are always kettles of whale and walrus cooking for good Eskimos who go there, while the bad go to a place where there is no food. When the Eskimo dies he goes to one of these two places, and his spears and knives are buried with him, so that he may help in the hunt-

ing. His friends put out the fire in his hut and
pull the fur hood over their heads in sign of
mourning. If they cry, every one near them must
cry too. He is buried by covering his body with
huge blocks of ice, and pouring water over the
blocks to freeze into a solid mass.

CHAPTER XV

ANOTHER ARCTIC WINTER

The winter passed at last. July came and the
"Advance" was still fast in the ice. The explorers
decided to try to reach the English squadron,
which they knew must be south of them, and get
fresh supplies, to use in case they should be forced
to remain another winter in the ice.

Dr. Kane felt he could not and would not desert the ship so early in the season. He took five
men with him and started out. They carried a
boat mounted on a sledge. His plan was to cross
the ice to open water, launch the boat, push
through the ice, secure supplies, and return.

After a fearful struggle with the ice the party
were forced to turn back. They reached the ship

FAST IN THE ICE

safely with the awful feeling that they would probably have to pass another winter in the ice. New
ice was already forming, and the poor little Arctic
plants were withered and dead.

Knowing they could go no farther north, the
explorers marked the spot by painting the name of
the vessel, "Advance," in huge letters on the face of
a great rock. Under the name they placed the
date, "1853-1854." Then they dug a hole in the
rock, in which they put a bottle. In the bottle was
a brief record of what they had done, and a list of
the men in the party.

The men were then called into the cabin, and
plans for the future discussed. Should they go or
stay? Eight decided to stay by the ship; the
rest wished to try to reach the Greenland settlements over the ice, and so to return home.

The stores were carefully divided, and the de-
parting men given as good an outfit as possible,
and a written assurance that if they failed and
came back to the ship they would be welcome.
They started away bravely and cheerily, dragging
their sledges behind them.

As soon as this home party had left, those who
remained were sadder than ever. Death seemed
to stare them in the face, but they must do their

best to ward it off. The sledges were taken out, and the men worked in the fearful cold quarrying out square frozen chunks of moss, dirt, grass, and sticks to cover the inside and outside of the cabin, and so keep out the cold. The floor of the cabin was covered with a plaster-of-Paris paste and oakum, over which canvas was spread. The outside of the brig was banked high with snow. A low moss-lined tunnel formed the entrance. The opening into this tunnel was covered with many thicknesses of curtains and skins.

From this place, which was almost like an Eskimo's hut, journeys were made to the filthy village of Etah, many miles over the ice. The people in the village received our men with the utmost hospitality, and although they had not much food themselves, they divided with Dr. Kane and his men.

There was now no fuel left, and what wood they burned was pulled from the sides of the brig. Daylight was leaving them, and the men's spirits fell as the sun dropped below the horizon. They were so gaunt and bony, and so racked with horrid diseases, that they could do no work. There were but twelve potatoes left, which were scraped and fed by the teaspoonful to the men most in

need of them.   To add to their distress, the men
who had left the ship returned, fainting with
hunger, frozen, and ill.

One day Dr. Kane found a boar's head, which
had been put away as a specimen. It was cooked,
and the meat from it kept the sick men alive for
several days. Hemp hawsers were burned to save
wood, but the smoke from them injured the lungs.
Manila ropes were used, but they burned too
fast.

In spite of the danger of leaving the sick, Dr.
Kane decided that he must get fresh food. Off he
started with his Eskimo boy, Hans. When only
fourteen miles away they were forced to crawl
into a deserted hut, close the door with blocks of
ice, and lie for hours, listening to the whirl and
rush of a snow-storm. They lunched from the raw
hind leg of a fox, drank coffee, slept, and woke
again. Floundering out, they plunged along a
short distance, until poor Hans, usually brave and
plucky, began to cry like a child.

It was still forty-six miles to the nearest settlement, and the journey had to be abandoned. Returning to the ship, they found the men no better.
At last one of the hunters came in with a rein-
deer. Not one atom of it was thrown away.

From horns to hoofs it was eaten up. A day or so later rabbits began to appear, and with the fresh food a little courage returned.

CHAPTER XVI

THE "ADVANCE" LEFT IN THE ICE

The long night finally drew toward its close, and daylight began to appear. The ship, which was still water tight, though much of her timber had been used for fire-wood, must now be given up. It was decided to make one final exploration over the ice, then abandon the search, and arrange for a homeward journey by sledges and small boats.

Dr. Kane induced the natives to carry him on this journey on their sledges. The floor of the sledge was made of slabs of frozen meat, across which the guns were laid, and the whole covered with a bearskin. When food was needed the men turned the sledge up side down and chopped off some of the meat floor of the sledge with an ax.

After exploring the ice in various directions,

climbing the highest icebergs and glaciers to search for traces of life, and finding none, the party returned to the vessel and began active preparations for the homeward journey. The men set to work with fresh vigor. Moccasins and boots were made, sleeping and provision bags were prepared of canvas, curtains, blankets, and skins.

They still had flour. Bread was baked, pounded to crumbs, and packed into the bags, which had been covered with pitch and tar to keep out the water. Other bags were filled with tallow and pork fat and bean soup frozen into solid chunks.

Three poor boats, one of which was to be used for firewood, were mounted on sledges. The precious instruments, and more precious food, were carefully stored away. Guns were distributed, cooking-pans fastened in place, and the sullen, discontented men unwillingly slipped their rueraddies over their heads, and on the 17th of May started from the stanch but dismantled little vessel.

Since there were only men enough to move the boats one at a time a mile a day, many trips had to be made back and forth to the ship, with a night's rest and a supper between each trip. When the time came for the last trip the men gathered for prayers, and then leaving the "Advance" to her fate in the ice, they sadly turned away to face thirteen hundred miles of suffering and privation.

CHAPTER XVII

HOME AGAIN

In due time they reached Etah, where the inhabitants were living a gypsy life out of doors, though the thermometer stood at five degrees below zero. Screaming and yelling, eating ràw birds, and tumbling over each other like puppies, these people were disgusting but hospitable.

For six hundred miles from Etah the road over the ice was well known. Snowstorms blocked their path, the dogs sickened and died, the ice began to soften. The men were snow-blind, and great masses of ice and rocks fell in unending din and danger all about them. Every sign pointed to open water. Again and again the sledges broke through the ice, and landed men and dogs alike, together with the precious journals, in the icy water.

At last the long journey was completed. The

Eskimo guides were given presents of soap, knives, files, and saws, and weeping and wailing and wiping their dirty faces on bird-skin handkerchiefs they returned homeward. Our explorers launched their boats, and with all flags thrown to the breeze, began their water journey.

A fearful gale delayed them, ice closed about the boats, the food supply grew very low, but they weathered all the storms, and after one or two stops where birds were thick or a seal was caught, they struggled bravely on.

On the 1st of August the glad cry of land was heard, and when as they approached the coast an oil-boat was seen

ESKIMO AND SLEDGE

and recognized, the men broke down, and cried and called and raved as if they had gone mad.

The sailors on the oil-boat told them that traces of Franklin's party had been discovered a thousand miles south of where they had been.

At Upernavik they took a ship for home, carrying with them nothing but their little boat, the "Faith," their journals, and the ragged clothes on their backs. Touching at Godhaven, they were surprised to see a steamer bearing the stars and stripes head into the harbor. Quickly the "Faith" was again launched, the Grinnell flag, which had been carried to the far south and the far north, floating above her. The men rowed out with a will, followed by all the boats of the settlement.

It was Captain Hartstene's expedition sent to rescue them. The question rang out loud and clear: "Is that Dr. Kane?"

"Yes"; and the men swarming to the rigging, cheered them to the echo.

So, after two years Dr. Kane returned to New York, to his family, and to the friend whose picture he had carried on his shoulders through all those dreary months. Ill, unpaid, and harassed, he soon left for England to see Lady Franklin, and to build up his shattered health.

Honors were now showered upon Dr. Kane. Great and learned men could not do enough to show him their admiration and respect, but disease had taken fast hold upon him.

Fleeing from English fogs Dr. Kane sailed to Cuba, hoping its mild climate would benefit him. His mother and brothers joined him in Havana, and one day while listening quietly to the reading of the Bible, which had been his constant companion through all his journeys, he slipped silently away to the land from which no traveler returns.

The removal of his body to his home in Philadelphia was one long series of sad ovations. All the cities from Havana to Philadelphia vied with one another to honor this man who had risked so much for science and humanity.

Would you ask what Dr. Kane accomplished? One glance at the great volumes of observations of tides and weather and climate and ice structure proves how faithful and persistent he was. His study of animals, birds, plants, and human customs shows how carefully observant he was. The maps he drew, the result of thousands of miles of travel by sea and land, on foot, by sledges, and by boat, illustrate his deep interest in science. His unwavering devotion to the search for Sir John Franklin and his party proves his unfailing love for humanity.

Dr. Kane exemplified in his life what courage, fortitude, patience, and good sense can do in the face of the severest trials, and we honor him as much for what he was as for what he did. Scores of other men have risked and lost their lives in those dreary seas, whose secret has not yet been discovered, but not one of them all has given greater proof of his worth as a man than did Elisha Kent Kane.

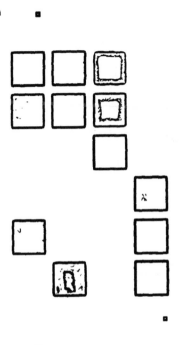

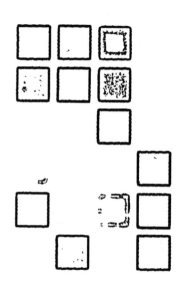